THORNTON W. BURGESS

THORNTON W. BURGESS
A DESCRIPTIVE BOOK BIBLIOGRAPHY

By

Wayne W. Wright

Sandwich, Massachusetts
The Thornton W. Burgess Society
1979

LCCN H.C. - 78-64641
ISBN H.C. - 0-88492-028-3

Illustrations from Little, Brown editions of
Burgess Books with permission of
Little, Brown and Company, Boston, Mass.

William S. Sullwold Publishing Inc.
Taunton, Massachusetts

TABLE OF CONTENTS

AN INTRODUCTION TO THE WORLD OF
THORNTON W. BURGESS

When Old Mother West Wind first came down from the Purple Hills to the Green Meadows in a 1910 collection of children's stories bearing her name, the author, Thornton W. Burgess, felt that his well of tales about her and her animal friends had run dry. How wrong he was, for from 1910 to his death in 1965 at the age of 91, this well was to produce over 70 full-scale books, more than 100 picture and paper books, 15,000 daily newspaper Bedtime Stories, and many other magazine stories, articles, and poems.

Little, Brown and Company of Boston published the original editions of 60 of Burgess's full-scale books, including eight series and several individual titles. Grosset & Dunlap of New York, through arrangements with Little, Brown, reissued 51 of the books and brought out several more original editions. In 1977, Grosset & Dunlap brought out 40 of the books again in new library bindings. Over the years, other publishing companies have brought out picture books and small paper booklets.

Burgess began his writing career with the sole purpose being to entertain children. He used characters and settings that were familiar to him — animals of meadow, forest, and pool. After becoming well-established as a children's author, Burgess continually infused facts about nature and the ways of wild creatures into the plots, under the belief that the story was the best method of conveying information to a child's mind. Instilling in children a healthy respect for nature became an important purpose of the books.

Teaching proper behavior was always a secondary goal of the books. Children identify with the main character of each book, and as the animals, who all have a moral sense, learn right and wrong from experience, Burgess expected the children to learn right and wrong from the animals.

Burgess characters are all representative of their kind. Some of them are personifications of inanimate objects and abstract concepts (such as Old Mother West Wind, the Merry Little Breezes, Mistress Spring, and Old Mother Nature). The majority of them typify species of animal life. Nearly every kind of North American mammal and bird is found as a Burgess character and given a Burgess name. Peter Rabbit, Grandfather Frog, Granny and Reddy Fox, Jimmy Skunk, Sammy Jay, and the rest live out the adventures found in the books.

Burgess animal stories readily lend themselves to illustration, and many artists have taken a hand at depicting the Burgess world. In illustrating the first four books of the Mother West Wind Series, George F. Kerr started the tradition of the animals wearing clothes. Harrison Cady, whose illustrations appeared in the books from 1913 to 1968, created the accepted image of the Burgess world. Through his humorous drawings, which had obvious departures from the text with humanizing elements, children came to know what the Green Forest and Green Meadows folk look like. The famous nature artist Louis Agassiz Fuertes did the illustrations for five Burgess books dealing with natural history during his middle period when he worked on assignments for books, magazines, and governmental publications. During the 1950's when there was a demand for realistic art in nature books, Phoebe Erickson gave a natural but lovable air to the illustrations. Others have made their unique contributions to the drawings, but by far the best known and best loved by Burgess fans are those of Harrison Cady, who at the end of his career was asked to reillustrate the Golden Anniversary editions of three Mother West Wind books.

In 1960, five years before his death, Thornton Burgess completed his last book — his own autobiography, *Now I Remember*. Little, Brown and Company had been urging him to write it for years, and the book of reminiscenes, heralded with great fanfare, made the perfect summation of Burgess's long and successful career.

It is not only the reissues and continual sales of the books that keep Burgess's memory alive. The Laughing Brook Education Center and Wildlife Sanctuary has been established at Burgess's home in Hampden, Massachusetts by the Massachusetts Audubon Society to continue his goals of conserving wildlife and educating the public in nature's ways. The citizens of Sandwich, Massachusetts, Burgess's birthplace, have created a Burgess museum and the Thornton W. Burgess Society dedicated to inspiring in youth a reverence for wildlife and promoting the continued use of Thornton W. Burgess books for young children.

A DESCRIPTIVE BIBLIOGRAPHY OF BOOKS BY THORNTON W. BURGESS

This bibliography of the books by Thornton W. Burgess had its inception in a seminar paper done for the course "The History of Children's Literature in America" at the School of Library and Information Science, State University of New York at Albany (1974). It gives a description of the first edition of each full-scale book and the other American editions of each, arranged by series with single books treated as a series of one. The series are arranged chronologically by the date of the first volume of the series. Later editions are listed chronologically after the first edition.

Books that are collections of or selections from members of a series are listed with the series unless they properly belong to another series (e.g. *Mother West Wind Stories to Read Aloud* is listed with the Read Aloud Books with a reference from the Mother West Wind Series).

The descriptions given are as close to the first printings as possible, with changes in later printings of the edition given in notes and in series introductions. The entry for each book can have up to eight parts as follows:

I. Transcription of the title page. Lower and upper case letters appear in the title page transcription in the way they appear on the title page. No distinction is made in the size of lettering or kind of printing. (If a kind of print is used in a certain manner throughout a series, it is noted in the series introduction.) A slash (/) indicates the end of one line of type on the title page. Information given in brackets indicates a word description of an illustration or symbol. The term "rule" means a straight line across the page.

II. Important information from the verso of the title page. Publication dates from other sources are placed here.

III. Collation — paging, illustrations, and size. Under paging, a leaf (1.) is both sides of a sheet of paper. A page is one side only. The letters p.l. stand for preliminary leaf or leaves, unnumbered leaves at the beginning of a book. The front matter is often numbered in lower case Roman numerals. The text of a book usually has a separate numbering system in Arabic numerals. The last unnumbered page in a numbering system is given in brackets. For example, 1 p.1., [4]-100p. means that the book has one preliminary leaf. The next four pages are unnumbered but would be pages 1-4. The first numbered page is 5. The text ends on page 100 with no indication of any blank pages after that.

There has been an attempt to give the number of full-page plates or illustrations. A plate has nothing printed on the verso. A full-page illustration has text printed on its other side. Colors used are generally noted.

The height and width of the page itself are given in centimeters. (Where only one number is given, it is the height.)

IV.   Binding. Included here can be cover material and its color, color of lettering, cover illustration, dust wrapper [d.w.], and end papers.

V.   Essential information from the preface, foreword, or introduction.

VI.   Dedication.

VII.   Contents — number of chapters and the subject matter or basic plot of the book.

VIII.   Note — giving historical or other background on the book. There may be more than one note.

Following the major section on the full-scale books comes a descriptive list of the picture books and small paper booklets. This list, arranged in the same manner, gives a full bibliographic citation for each book, with later editions following chronologically, giving differences between the later and first editions. Pagination given in leaves or bracketed means the pages of the book are unnumbered. Generally only the number of pages is given. Notes on the book are given under the citation. Books marked with an asterisk indicate collections of or selections from the members of the series.

Abbreviations used in this bibliography are:

b&w — black and white	trans. — translated
bds. — boards	MWW — Mother West Wind Series
c. — copyright	BS — Boy Scout Series
cm. — centimeters	BSB — The Bedtime Story-Books
col. — color	GM — Green Meadow Series
d.w. — dust wrapper	NH — Burgess Natural History Books
ed. — edition or editor	for Children
front. — frontispiece	GF — Green Forest Series
full-col. — full-color	SP — Smiling Pool Series
G&D — Grosset & Dunlap	LCC — Little Color Classics
illus. — illustration(s), illustrated, or	NS — Books of Nature Stories
illustrator	WB — Wonder Books
incl. — including	WRA — Wonder Read Aloud Books
l. — leaf or leaves	GH — *Good Housekeeping*
p. — page(s)	PHJ — *People's Home Journal*
p.l. — preliminary leaf or leaves	BtS — Burgess's syndicated *Bedtime Stories*
part. — partly	column
photo. — photographs	Delin. — *Delineator*
pl. — plates	SN — *Saint Nicholas*
pub. — published	SR — *Springfield Republican*

Most of the books listed in this bibliography have been examined first-hand. Information has also come from the following sources:

National Union Catalog
Cumulative Book Index
Publisher's Trade List Annual
Catalogue of Copyright Entries
English Catalogue of Books
People's Home Journal volumes at the New York Public Library
Thornton W. Burgess file at the Springfield (Mass.) Public Library
"A Bibliography of Thornton Burgess," compiled privately for the University of Wisconsin Memorial Library by John Neu (about 1959), 19p.
"Bibliography of Books Written by Thornton W. Burgess" by Ralph Titcomb in *The Cape Cod Story of Thornton W. Burgess* by Russell A. Lovell, Jr. (Sandwich, Mass., Thornton W. Burgess Centennial Committee, 1974), pp. 95-104.
Thornton W. Burgess: A Magazine Bibliography by Michael Dowhan, Jr. (Williamstown, Mass., printed by Chapel Hill Press, 1977), 60p.

Especially good book collections used in compiling this bibliography are: The Roy W. Oppegard collection owned by the University of Wisconsin Memorial Library; books at the New York State Library at Albany; books on display at the Thornton W. Burgess Museum, Deacon Eldred House, Sandwich, Mass.; and Burgess's own library at the Laughing Brook Education Center and Wildlife Sanctuary, Hampden, Mass.

Acknowledgments must go to the following, who were of great aid to the compiler while working on this project.

Mrs. Gerald S. Wright (my mother, who during my childhood encouraged my interest in children's books)
David Mitchell (professor of children's literature at the school of Library and Information Science, State University of New York at Albany)
Mr. and Mrs. Ralph Titcomb (who allowed me to use their Burgess collection. Ralph gave me the information he compiled for the first extensive bibliography. Nancy, Director of the Thornton W. Burgess Society, helped in innumerable ways.)
Michael Dowhan, Jr. and Michael Dowhan, Sr. (Burgess magazine bibliographers and book collectors).
Major Benton (Director of the Massachusett's Audubon Society's Laughing Brook Education and Wildlife Sanctuary, Hampden, Massachusetts) and the Laughing Brook staff.
Marilyn Bailey (my sister, always with an eye open for Burgess books)
Judie Rothermel (also alert for Burgess material)
Carl Waldman (who helped with the proofreading)
Edward C. Robinson (photographer of the Burgess book covers and illustrations)

To these helpers and to the memory of my grandmother, Luella A. Smith, who read Burgess books to me as a child, this book is dedicated.

VARIETIES OF BURGESS BOOK END PAPERS

End papers from *On the Green Meadows*. Boston, Little, Brown, c.1944. Illus. by Harrison Cady.

Map "Burgessville, U.S.A." by Phoebe Erickson from end papers of *Baby Animal Stories*. New York, Grosset & Dunlap, c. 1949.

GROSSET & DUNLAP SERIES END PAPERS

Grosset & Dunlap used three different end papers illustrated with Harrison Cady figures for its editions of the Burgess series. The end paper numbers in this bibliography refer to these three styles

1.   This style, printed at first in light green without a border, was used in the Mother West Wind Series, the first series Grosset issued. It was then used with a border in the Green Meadow, Green Forest, and Smiling Pool Series, and was printed in dark green.

2.   Printed in green, this style was used in Grosset's editions of the Bedtime Story-Books. Much less common than #3 (which is the one given to the Bedtime Story-Books in this bibliography), only a few books using it have been examined.

3.   The most common of the three, this style end paper was used in Grosset's Bedtime Story-Books and The Wishing-Stone Stories. It replaced #1 in the Mother West Wind, Green Meadow, Green Forest, and Smiling Pool series. It was for several years printed in green, and finally changed to black. The black variation is found in all the Grosset series presently in print.

THE BRIDE'S PRIMER (1905)

The BRIDE'S PRIMER / BEING A SERIES OF QUAINT PARODIES / on the ways of BRIDES and their MISADVENTURES interlarded / with USEFUL HINTS / for their AD-/ VANTAGE [flower design] / text by THORNTON W. BURGESS and others, with / an essay by TOM MASSON and pictures by / [design] F. STROTHMAN [design] / [rule] / Published by the Phelps Publishing Co. / For sale to the trade by Orange Judd Company, New York

- c.1905 Phelps Pub. Co.
- 31 l., 24 full-page illus., 31x22cm.
- gray paper on bds., brown lettering, gray and dark brown illus.
- "[This book is] in response to a heartfelt and widespread appeal . . . to rescue [the Bride] from chilly retirement of *Good Housekeeping's* bound files and back numbers and send her forth in a pretty book, a companion to other brides and brides-to-be."
- XXIV verses showing the foolish things new brides do. Each verse has a facing illus. A seven-page essay entitled "Being a Bride" follows.
- Burgess's first published book, the verses first appeared in *Good Housekeeping* magazine, two verses monthly from Jan.-Dec., 1905. The Neu bibliography lists both a regular edition and an edition deluxe.

Covers and title pages of various editions of *Old Mother West Wind*, Burgess's first animal story book.

OLD
MOTHER WEST WIND

BY
THORNTON W. BURGESS

Illustrated by George Kerr

BOSTON
LITTLE, BROWN, AND COMPANY

First Edition — 1910. Little, Brown, c.1910. Illus. by George Kerr.

BURGESS TRADE QUADDIES MARK

OLD
MOTHER WEST WIND

BY
THORNTON W. BURGESS

Illustrated by George Kerr

BOSTON
LITTLE, BROWN, AND COMPANY
1931

Title page and dust wrapper of a 1931 printing of the original Little, Brown edition. Illus. by George Kerr. The Burgess Quaddies trademark and the Little, Brown logo have been added to the title page.

School Edition — 1912. Little, Brown, c.1910. Illus. by George Kerr. This title page is from a 1915 printing.

Color Edition — 1914. Little, Brown, c.1910, 1914. Illus. by George Kerr.

Dust wrapper and title page of the Golden Anniversary Edition — 1960. Little, Brown, c.1910, renewed 1938, c.1960 by Thornton W. Burgess. Illus. by Harrison Cady.

BURGESS TRADE QUADDIES MARK

OLD
MOTHER WEST WIND

BY

THORNTON W. BURGESS

Illustrated by George Kerr

GROSSET & DUNLAP
Publishers   New York
By arrangement with Little, Brown and Company

Grosset & Dunlap library binding edition — 1977. Illus. by George Kerr.

MOTHER WEST WIND SERIES (1910-1918)

The beginning of the Burgess animal stories for children and the Mother West Wind Series came in 1910 when Burgess's four-year-old son, Thornton III, went visiting with his grandmother in Chicago. Each evening while the boy was away, his father wrote stories or verses and sent them to him. At the time Burgess did not intend them for publication, but later that year he had three of the stories printed in *Good Housekeeping* magazine, where he was an editor.

Soon a representative of the publishing firm of Little, Brown and Company of Boston visited *Good Housekeeping's* offices in Springfield, Massachusetts, and was shown some of Burgess's stories. The man asked Burgess to send some stories of the same type to Little, Brown with the idea of publishing them as a book. Burgess sent fourteen stories, all he had written, and soon Little, Brown asked for two more to fill out a volume. Burgess created two more stories, and the book came out in the fall of 1910 as *Old Mother West Wind*. It was immediately successful.

Burgess felt he had written all of the animal stories he knew, but the next year the publisher asked for more, so Burgess went on to write the stories for *Mother West Wind's Children*. The series eventually grew to include eight books.

A common motif in all the books in the series is Old Mother West Wind, the west wind personified, who comes down from the Purple Hills to the Green Meadows each morning bringing her children, the Merry Little Breezes, with her in a large sack. The Merry Little Breezes play on the Green Meadows all day while Mother West Wind goes out into the great world to turn the windmills and fill the sails of the ships at sea. The stories in the series are of two types — tales of the adventures of the Green Meadow and Green Forest animals and Burgess-created legends, fanciful explanations of natural phenomena usually put into the mouths of wise creatures such as Grandfather Frog. The stories in the last four books are nearly all of the legendary type.

The Little, Brown editions of the Mother West Wind Series began to be issued under the Burgess Quaddies trademark in 1915 with the fifth volume, *Mother West Wind "Why" Stories.* (The trademark was printed BURGESS TRADE QUADDIES MARK with the words "trade mark" in smaller print.) The books of the series issued after this and the reprintings of the earlier books all had the Burgess Quaddies trademark on the title page. The title page date was changed to correspond with the year of each reprinting. At some point they were issued with illustrated dust wrappers.

The first four books of the series were illustrated by George Kerr, and the last four by Harrison Cady. In 1960, to celebrate the golden anniversary of *Old Mother West Wind,* Little, Brown brought out an edition of the book newly illustrated by Harrison Cady. He later illustrated a new edition of *Mother West Wind's Children,* and finally in 1968, *Mother West Wind's Neighbors* was issued with Cady illustrations, leaving *Mother West Wind's Animal Friends* the only book in the series not to be published with Cady pictures.

The first printings of the Grosset & Dunlap editions of the Mother West Wind Series (as described in this bibliography) came out in 1940 and 1941 with covers of green cloth on boards, 17cm., 4 b&w pl. on glossy paper, and end papers (#1) of a light green variety with no border. Illustrated dust wrappers came on the books, with each member of the series in a different color. During World War II, this version of the books was issued with a statement on the title page about the wartime quality of the paper.

Later the covers were changed to blue paper on boards with the lettering and illustration stamped in black and light blue. Even later the cover illustration was dark blue on a blue cover. The four plates on glossy paper were eventually changed to four plates redrawn in line drawings on paper of the same quality as the paper of the text. The end papers have gone through several forms — end papers #1 done in dark green with border, and #3 done in green and later in black.

About 1962, Grosset & Dunlap issued the whole series in light green paper on board covers with no dust wrapper. The original dust wrapper illustrations were printed on the cover.

Most recently, in 1977, Grosset issued the series in library binding, tan covers, with cover titles of the first four books of the series preceded by the phrase "The Adventures of. . . ." The size was made uniform with the other 1977 series reprints — 19cm.

In some cases the cover illustration of the School Editions and the Grosset printings are different from the cover illustrations of the original Little, Brown editions, the picture having been exchanged with another one from the book. In these cases the title of the illustration is noted under each printing in the bibliography.

Many of the stories in the series first appeared in periodicals and newspapers and then were printed in the books. The "Why," "How," "When," and "Where" stories were collected from among those appearing in *Peoples Home Journal*. Wherever possible these original sources are indicated after the story titles in the descriptions with the following abbreviations:

Good Housekeeping — GH
People's Home Journal — PHJ
Bedtime Stories (the title of Burgess's syndicated newspaper story column) *— BtS*
Delineator — Delin.

The volumes in the series are:

1. Old Mother West Wind — 1910
2. Mother West Wind's Children — 1911
3. Mother West Wind's Animal Friends — 1912
4. Mother West Wind's Neighbors — 1913
5. Mother West Wind "Why" Stories — 1915
6. Mother West Wind "How" Stories — 1916
7. Mother West Wind "When" Stories — 1917
8. Mother West Wind "Where" Stories — 1918

————————————➤ •●• ◄————————————

1.   OLD MOTHER WEST WIND — 1910

A.   OLD / MOTHER WEST WIND / BY / THORNTON W. BURGESS / Illustrated by George Kerr / BOSTON / LITTLE, BROWN, AND COMPANY

- c.1910. Printers S. J. Parkhill & Co., Boston.

- 5 p.l., [3]-169p., 7 b&w pl. incl. front., 17x11cm.

- tan cloth on bds.; illus. stamped in black, green & red (a reversal of plate entitled " 'Where are you going in such a hurry, Striped Chipmunk?' asked Peter Rabbit."); lettering stamped in black and bordered in black.

- "To My Mother to whom I owe so much and to My Little Son whose love of stories inspired these tales this little volume is affectionately dedicated."

-    I.   Mrs. Redwing's Speckled Egg
    II.   Why Grandfather Frog Has No Tail
   III.   How Reddy Fox Was Surprised [*GH,* 50 (Apr. 1910), 482-4, with 2 illus. by George Kerr]
   IV.   Why Jimmy Skunk Wears Stripes
    V.   The Wilful Little Breeze
   VI.   Reddy Fox Goes Fishing
  VII.   Jimmy Skunk Looks for Beetles
  VIII.   Billy Mink's Swimming Party
   IX.   Peter Rabbit Plays a Joke [*GH,* 50 (June 1910), 741-3, 2 Kerr illus.]
    X.   How Sammy Jay Was Found Out
   XI.   Jerry Muskrat's Party

XII. Bobby Coon and Reddy Fox Play Tricks
XIII. Johnny Chuck Finds the Best Thing in the World [*GH*, 51 (July 1910), 62-4, 2 Kerr illus.]
XIV. Little Joe Otter's Slippery Slide
XV. The Tale of Tommy Trout Who Didn't Mind
XVII. Spotty the Turtle Wins a Race

- Burgess's second book to be published and his first animal story book. Of the six Kerr illustrations for these tales that appeared in *GH*, four are found among the illustrations for this book.

- The copies of this edition examined contained an advertisement for the sequel, *Mother West Wind's Children*. This reference to the next book was probably added later and not found in the first printings, since at the time of publication of *Old Mother West Wind* there were no plans for another book. Burgess claimed at that time, "I had written every last animal story I knew."*

- *Old Mother West Wind* came out in a School Edition, published by Little, Brown in 1912. The only difference from the above is that it contains only XV stories (153p.). Story XVI, "Spotty the Turtle Wins a Race," is deleted.

B. OLD / MOTHER WEST WIND / BY / THORNTON W. BURGESS / WITH ILLUSTRATIONS IN COLOR BY / GEORGE F. KERR / [pub. logo] / BOSTON / LITTLE, BROWN, AND COMPANY / 1914

- c.1910, 1914. Illus. ed. pub. Sept. 1914. Printers S. J. Parkhill & Co., Boston.

- 5 p.l., [2]-147p., 8 col. pl. incl. front., 24x17cm.

- blue cloth on bds., lettering and flower design stamped in gold, full-col. illus. pasted in center, bordered in gold.

- Same dedication and contents as 1A.

C. BURGESS ᵀᴿᴬᴰᴱ QUADDIES ᴹᴬᴿᴷ / [rule] / OLD / MOTHER WEST WIND / BY / THORNTON W. BURGESS / Illustrated by George Kerr / GROSSET & DUNLAP / Publishers   New York / By arrangement with Little, Brown and Company

- c.1910 [First pub. by G&D in 1940].

- Same collation as 1A except only 4 b&w pl. incl. front.

- green cloth on bds.; illus. stamped in black and blue; lettering stamped in black and bordered in black; d.w. with full-col. illus.; end papers #1.

- Same dedication and contents as 1A.

- The binding of about 1962 has a redrawn version of the cover illus. in 1A, but not reversed. The 1977 library binding has cover title *The Adventures of Old Mother West Wind*.

---

* Thornton W. Burgess, *Now I Remember* (Boston, Little, Brown, 1960), p. 131.

D. OLD MOTHER / WEST WIND / Golden Anniversary Edition / By / THORNTON W. BURGESS / With Illustrations by Harrison Cady / LITTLE, BROWN [pub. logo] BOSTON TORONTO

- c.1910, 1938, 1960 [pub. by Little, Brown in 1960].
- 5 p.l., [2]-140p., 7 illus. in full-col. (6 full-page, incl. front. and 1 two-page spread) and many b&w illus., 21x16cm.
- green cloth on bds.; lettering and illus. stamped in gold; d.w. with same col. illus. as two-page spread.
- Same dedication as 1A.
- Same contents as 1A except stories II & III are reversed and stories VII & VIII are reversed.
- This edition, newly illustrated by Harrison Cady, contains a picture of Old Mother West Wind who, in the past, was seldom drawn.

2. MOTHER WEST WIND'S CHILDREN — 1911

A. MOTHER WEST WIND'S / CHILDREN / BY / THORNTON W. BURGESS / Author of "Old Mother West Wind" / Illustrated by George Kerr / BOSTON / LITTLE, BROWN, AND COMPANY / 1911

- c.1911. Printers S. J. Parkhill & Co., Boston.
- 5 p.l., [3]-243p., 7 b&w pl. incl. front., 17x11cm.
- tan cloth on bds.; illus. stamped in black, green & blue; lettering stamped in black and bordered in black.
- "To All the·Little Friends of Johnny Chuck and Reddy Fox, and to All Who Love the Green Meadows and the Smiling Pool, The Laughing Brook and the Merry Little Breezes, this little book is dedicated."
- I.   Danny Meadow Mouse Learns Why His Tail is Short [*PHJ*, June 1911]
  II.   Why Reddy Fox has no Friends
  III. Why Peter Rabbit's Ears are Long [*GH*, 52 (Apr. 1911), 509-11, 2 Kerr illus.]
  IV.   Reddy Fox Disobeys [*GH*, 52 (Mar. 1911), 393-95, under title "Reddy Fox Barks at the Moon," 2 Kerr illus.]
  V.   Striped Chipmunk's Pockets [*GH*, 53 (July 1911), 126-8, 1 Kerr illus.]
  VI.   Reddy Fox, the Boaster [*GH*, 53 (Oct. 1911), 517-19, 1 Kerr illus.]
  VII. Johnny Chuck's Secret
  VIII. Johnny Chuck's Great Fight
  IX.   Mr. Toad's Old Suit [*GH*, 53 (Nov. 1911), 667-9, 1 Kerr illus.]
  X.   Grandfather Frog Gets Even [*GH*, 52 (May 1911), 635-7, 1 Kerr illus.]
  XI.   The Disappointed Bush
  XII. Why Bobby Coon Washes His Food [*PHJ*, Oct. 1911]
  XIII. The Merry Little Breezes Have a Busy Day
  XIV. Why Hooty the Owl Does not Play on the Green Meadows
  XV.   Danny Meadow Mouse Learns to Laugh

- Burgess's second animal story book. The tales in *GH* are somewhat shorter than the ones in the book. Of the 8 Kerr illus. in *GH*, 5 appeared in the book, but a rare one of Mother Nature did not.

- *Mother West Wind's Children* came out in a School Edition, published by Little, Brown in 1912. It contains only stories I-X (168p.).

B.   BURGESS <u>TRADE</u> QUADDIES <u>MARK</u> / [rule] / MOTHER WEST WIND'S / CHILDREN / BY / THORNTON W. BURGESS / Author of "Old Mother West Wind" / Illustrated by George Kerr / GROSSET & DUNLAP / Publishers   New York / By arrangement with Little, Brown and Company

- c.1911 [1st pub. by G&D in 1940].

- Same collation as 2A except only 4 b&w pl. incl. front.

- green cloth on bds.; illus. stamped in black & blue; lettering stamped in black and bordered in black; d.w. with full-col. illus.; end papers #1.

- Same dedication and contents as 2A.

- The G&D library binding format of 1977 has cover title *The Adventures of Mother West Wind's Children*.

C.   MOTHER / WEST WIND'S / CHILDREN / New Illustrated Edition / by / THORNTON W. BURGESS / With Illustrations by Harrison Cady / [pub. logo] / LITTLE, BROWN AND COMPANY • BOSTON • TORONTO

- c.1911, 1939, 1962 [Pub. by Little, Brown in 1962].

- 5 p.l., [3]-156p., 9 full-col. illus. (8 full-page incl. front. and 1 two-page spread) and many b&w illus., 21x16cm.

- blue cloth on bds.; lettering and illus. stamped in gold; d.w. with same col. illus. as the two-page spread.

- Same dedication and contents as 2A.

- The two Cady illus. of Mother Nature in this book are the same as the figure called Mother West Wind in the companion book *Old Mother West Wind; Golden Anniversary Edition*.

3.   MOTHER WEST WIND'S
ANIMAL FRIENDS — 1912

A.   MOTHER WEST WIND'S / ANIMAL FRIENDS / BY / THORNTON W. BURGESS / Author of "Old Mother West Wind," and / "Mother West Wind's Children" / Illustrated by George Kerr / BOSTON / LITTLE, BROWN, AND COMPANY / 1912

- c.1912. Pub. Sept. 1912. The Colonial Press, C. H. Simonds & Co., Boston.

- 5 p.l., [3]-221p., 6 b&w pl. incl. front., 17x11cm.

- tan cloth on bds.; illus. stamped in black, red & yellow from plate entitled "Reddy strutted out in front of him. 'Who are you?' he demanded."; lettering stamped in black, bordered in black.

- "In tender, loving, reverent memory of my mother, who loved little children and was beloved of them, and to whom I owe a debt of affection and gratitude beyond my power to pay."

- I.   The Merry Little Breezes Save the Green Meadows
  II.   The Stranger in the Green Forest
  III.   How Prickly Porky Got His Quills
  IV.   Peter Rabbit's Egg Rolling [*Delin.*, 79 (Apr. 1912), 356]
  V.   How Johnny Chuck Ran Away [*BtS* (Feb. 6-8, 1912)]
  VI.   Peter Rabbit's Run For Life [*BtS* (Feb. 9-10, 1912)]
  VII.   A Joker Fooled
  VIII.   The Fuss in the Big Pine
  IX.   Johnny Chuck Finds a Use for His Back Door [*BtS* (Mar. 22-24, 1912)]
  X.   Billy Mink Goes Dinnerless
  XI.   Grandfather Frog's Journey [*BtS* (May 13, 1912)]
  XII.   Why Blacky the Crow Wears Mourning [*PHJ* (Sept. 1912), 2 +]
  XIII.   Striped Chipmunk Fools Peter Rabbit
  XIV.   Jerry Muskrat's New House [*BtS* (Apr. 8-12, 1912)]
  XV.   Peter Rabbit's Big Cousin [*BtS* (Apr. 12, 1912)]

- The only member of the Mother West Wind Series that did not come out in an edition illustrated by Harrison Cady.

- *Mother West Wind's Animal Friends* came out in a School Edition, pub. by Little, Brown in 1912 (159p.), stories I-XI only, 4 b&w pl., cover illus. from plate entitled "Come with us to the Big River fishing."

B.   BURGESS TRADE QUADDIES MARK / [rule] / MOTHER WEST WIND'S / ANIMAL FRIENDS / BY / THORNTON W. BURGESS / Author of "Old Mother West Wind" and / "Mother West Wind's Children" / Illustrated by George Kerr / GROSSET & DUNLAP / Publishers New York / By arrangement with Little, Brown and Company

- c.1912 [1st pub. by G&D in 1940].

- Same collation as 3A except only 4 b&w pl. incl. front.

- green cloth on bds.; illus. stamped in black & blue from plate entitled "Reddy strutted out in front of him. 'Who are you?' he demanded."; lettering stamped in black and bordered in black; d.w. with full-col. illus., end papers #1.

- Same dedication and contents as 3A.

- Later G&D printing (green paper on bds., no d.w., about 1962) has cover illus. from plate entitled "Come with us to the Big River fishing." The G&D library binding format of 1977 has cover title *The Adventures of Mother West Wind's Animal Friends*.

4.   MOTHER WEST WIND'S NEIGHBORS — 1913

A.   MOTHER WEST WIND'S / NEIGHBORS / BY / THORNTON W. BURGESS / Author of "Old Mother West Wind," / "Mother West Wind's Animal Friends," etc. / Illustrated by George Kerr / BOSTON / LITTLE, BROWN, AND COMPANY / 1913

- c.1913. Pub. Sept. 1913. The Colonial Press, C. H. Simonds & Co., Boston.

- 5 p.l., [3]-223p., 6 b&w pl. incl. front., 17x11cm.

- tan cloth on bds.; illus. stamped in green, blue & black from plate entitled " 'Chugarum!' began Grandfather Frog, in a very deep voice.''; lettering stamped in black and bordered in black.

- "To the silent partner whose faith, helpful criticisms and never failing optimism are a perpetual source of inspiration, MY WIFE.''

- I.   Why Johnny Chuck Does not Like Blacky the Crow (*Todays* (Nov. 1912), 47]
  II.   Unc' Billy Possum Arrives [*BtS* (May 6-9, 1912)]
  III.   Why Ol' Mistah Buzzard Has a Bald Head [*BtS* (July 15-16, 1912)]
  IV.   Hooty the Owl Gets Even [*BtS* (Mar. 11-12, 1912)]
  V.   Happy Jack Squirrel's Stolen Nuts
  VI.   Why Sammy Jay Cries "Thief" [*Todays* (Aug. 1913), 39]
  VII.   The Most Beautiful Thing in the World [*PHJ* (Aug. 1912), 2]
  VIII.   Old Mrs. Possum's Big Pocket [*BtS* (June 13-15, 1912)]
  IX.   Why Peter Rabbit Wears a White Patch
  X.   Who Stole the Eggs of Mrs. Grouse [*BtS* (May 1-4, 1912)]
  XI.   How Digger the Badger Came to the Green Meadows [*BtS* (June 17-21, 1912)]
  XII.   Why Mistah Mocker is the Best Loved of all the Birds [*BtS* (Nov. 15-16, 1912)]
  XIII.   The Impudence of Mr. Snake
  XIV.   Peter Rabbit's First Snow [*BtS* (Jan. 3-6, 1913)]
  XV.   Mrs. Grouse Goes to Bed [*BtS* (Jan. 8-9, 1913)]

- *Mother West Wind's Neighbors* came out in a School Edition, published by Little, Brown in 1913. It contained only stories I-XI (168p.), 4 b&w pl., cover illus. from plate entitled "He made the leaves fly in every direction."

B.   BURGESS <u>TRADE</u> QUADDIES <u>MARK</u> / [rule] / MOTHER WEST WIND'S / NEIGHBORS / BY / THORNTON W. BURGESS / Author of "Old Mother West Wind," and / "Mother West Wind's Children" / Illustrated by George Kerr / GROSSET & DUNLAP / Publishers   New York / By arrangement with Little, Brown and Company

- c.1913 [1st pub. by G&D in 1940].

- Same collation as 4A except only 4 b&w pl. incl. front.

- green cloth on bds.; illus. stamped in black and blue from plate entitled " 'Chugarum!' began Grandfather Frog in a very deep voice.''; lettering stamped in black and bordered in black; d.w. with full-col. illus.; end papers #1.

- Same dedication and contents as 4A.

- Later G&D printing (green paper on bds., no d.w., about 1962) has cover illus. from plate entitled "Straight up to the hollow stump went Shadow the Weasel." The G&D library binding of 1977 has cover title *The Adventures of Mother West Wind's Neighbors*.

C.   MOTHER / WEST WIND'S / NEIGHBORS / New Illustrated Edition / by / THORNTON W. BURGESS / With Illustrations by Harrison Cady / Foreword by Charles E. Roth / of the Massachusetts Audubon Society / [pub.

logo] / LITTLE, BROWN AND COMPANY • BOSTON • TORONTO

- c.1913, 1941, 1968 [Pub. by Little, Brown in 1968].

- [vi]-xii, [2]-148p., 8 full-col. pl. incl. front., many b&w illus., 21x16cm.

- red-orange cloth on bds.; lettering & illus. stamped in gold; d.w. with full-col. illus. (from end papers of *The Crooked Little Path* by Thornton W. Burgess. Boston, Little, Brown, 1946).

- Same dedication and contents as 4A.

- The last Burgess book to be illustrated by Harrison Cady. Several of the drawings were taken from previous editions of Burgess books.

5. MOTHER WEST WIND "WHY" STORIES — 1915

A. BURGESS <u>TRADE</u> QUADDIES <u>MARK</u> / [rule] / MOTHER WEST WIND / "WHY" STORIES / BY / THORNTON W. BURGESS / Author of "Old Mother West Wind," and / "The Bed Time Story-Books." / Illustrations in Color by / HARRISON CADY / [pub. logo] / BOSTON / LITTLE, BROWN, AND COMPANY / 1915

- c.1915. Printers S. J. Parkhill & Co., Boston.

- 4 p.l., [3]-230p., 8 pl. done in green, red, & black incl. front., 17x11cm.

- tan cloth on bds.; illus. stamped in black, green & red; lettering stamped in black and bordered in black.

- The stories are all of legendary type, explaining natural phenomena. Grandfather Frog tells tales of when the world was young and "why" Mother Nature gave various animals their distinctive characteristics.

- I.   Why Striped Chipmunk is Proud of His Stripes [*PHJ* (July 1913), 17, under title "How Chipmunk Came By His Stripes"]
  II.   Why Peter Rabbit Cannot Fold His Hands [*PHJ* (Aug. 1913), 20]
  III.   Why Unc' Billy Possum Plays Dead [*PHJ* (Dec. 1913), 23]
  IV.   Why Reddy Fox Wears Red [*PHJ* (May 1913), 24, under title "Why Reddy Fox Wears a Red Coat"]
  V.   Why Jimmy Skunk Never Hurries [*PHJ* (Oct. 1914), 42]
  VI.   Why Sammy Jay Has a Fine Coat [*PHJ* (Jul. 1914), 26]
  VII.   Why Jerry Muskrat Builds His House in the Water [*PHJ* (Nov. 1913), 38]
  VIII.   Why Old Man Coyote Has Many Voices [*PHJ* (Aug. 1914), 26]
  IX.   Why Miner the Mole Lives Under Ground [*PHJ* (Jan. 1914), 30]
  X.   Why Mr. Snake Cannot Wink [*PHJ* (Sept. 1913), 22]
  XI.   Why Bobby Coon Has Rings on His Tail [*PHJ* (Oct. 1913), 42]
  XII.   Why There is a Black Head in the Buzzard Family [*BtS* (Nov. 20, 1912), under title "Why Ol' Mistah Buzzard's Cousin Has a Black Head"]
  XIII.   Why Buster Bear Appears to Have No Tail [*PHJ* (Nov. 1914), 38]
  XIV.   Why Flitter the Bat Flies at Night [*PHJ* (June 1914), 30]
  XV.   Why Spotty the Turtle Carries His House With Him [*PHJ* (Sept. 1914), 30]

XVI.   Why Paddy the Beaver Has A Broad Tail [*PHJ* (May 1914), 34, under title "How Mr. Beaver Got His Broad Tail"]

B.   BURGESS <u>TRADE</u> QUADDIES <u>MARK</u> / [rule] / MOTHER WEST WIND / "WHY" STORIES / BY / THORNTON W. BURGESS / Illustrations by / HARRISON CADY / GROSSET & DUNLAP / PUBLISHERS   NEW YORK / By arrangement with Little, Brown, and Company

- c.1915 [1st pub. by G&D in 1941].

- Same collation as 5A except only 4 b&w pl. incl. front.

- Same binding as 5A except green cloth on bds., illus. stamped in black & blue, d.w. with full-col. illus., end papers #1.

- Same contents as 5A.

6.   MOTHER WEST WIND "HOW" STORIES — 1916

A.   BURGESS <u>TRADE</u> QUADDIES <u>MARK</u> / [rule] / MOTHER WEST WIND / "HOW" STORIES / BY / THORNTON W. BURGESS / Author of "Old Mother West Wind," / "The Bed Time Story-Books," etc. / Illustrations in Color by / HARRISON CADY / [pub. logo] / BOSTON / LITTLE, BROWN, AND COMPANY / 1916

- c.1916. Pub. Sept. 1916 The Colonial Press, C. H. Simonds Co., Boston.

- [vii]-viii, 1 l., [3]-228p., 8 pl. done in green, orange, & black incl. front., 17x11cm.

- tan cloth on bds.; illus. stamped in black, green & red; lettering stamped in black and bordered in black.

- "To the cause of conservation of wild life and to increase of love for our little friends of the Green Forest and the Green Meadows through awakened interest in them and a better understanding of their value to us as faithful workers in carrying out the plans of wise Old Mother Nature, this little book is dedicated."

- I.   How Old King Eagle Won His White Head [*PHJ* (Aug. 1915), 26]
  II.   How Old Mr. Mink Taught Himself to Swim [*PHJ* (Apr. 1914), 38]
  III.   How Old Mr. Toad Learned to Sing [*PHJ* (June 1915), 30]
  IV.   How Old Mr. Crow Lost His Double Tongue [*PHJ* (Apr. 1915), 38]
  V.   How Howler the Wolf Got His Name [*PHJ* (Nov. 1915), 34]
  VI.   How Old Mr. Squirrel Became Thrifty [*PHJ* (June 1913), 23]
  VII.   How Lightfoot the Deer Learned to Jump [*PHJ* (Dec. 1914), 34]
  VIII. How Mr. Flying Squirrel Almost Got Wings [*PHJ* (Sept. 1915), 30]
  IX.   How Mr. Weasel Was Made an Outcast [*PHJ* (Mar. 1915), 42]
  X.   How the Eyes of Old Mr. Owl Became Fixed [*PHJ* (May 1915), 34]
  XI.   How It Happens Johnny Chuck Sleeps All Winter [*PHJ* (Jan. 1915), 30]
  XII.   How Old Mr. Otter Learned to Slide [*PHJ* (Mar. 1914)]
  XIII. How Drummer the Woodpecker Came by His Red Cap [*PHJ* (Feb. 1914), 34]
  XIV.   How Old Mr. Tree Toad Found Out How to Climb [*PHJ* (Jul. 1915), 26]

XV.   How Old Mr. Heron Learned Patience [*PHJ* (Feb. 1916), 38]
XVI.   How Tufty the Lynx Happens to Have a Stump of a Tail [*PHJ* (Jul. 1915), 26]

B.   BURGESS <u>TRADE</u> QUADDIES <u>MARK</u> / [rule] / MOTHER WEST WIND / "HOW" STORIES / BY / THORNTON W. BURGESS / Illustrations by / HARRISON CADY / GROSSET & DUNLAP / PUBLISHERS   NEW YORK / By arrangement with Little, Brown, and Company

- c.1916 [1st pub. by G&D in 1941].

- Same collation as 6A except only 4 b&w pl. incl. front.

- Same binding as 6A except for green cloth on bds., illus. stamped in black and blue, d.w. with full-col. illus., end papers #1.

- Same dedication and contents as 6A.

7.   MOTHER WEST WIND
"WHEN" STORIES — 1917

A.   BURGESS <u>TRADE</u> QUADDIES <u>MARK</u> / [rule] / MOTHER WEST WIND / "WHEN" STORIES / BY / THORNTON W. BURGESS / Author of "Old Mother West Wind," / "The Bed Time Story-Books," etc. / Illustrations in Color by / HARRISON CADY / [pub. logo] / BOSTON / LITTLE, BROWN, AND COMPANY / 1917

- c.1917. Pub. Sept. 1917. The Colonial Press, C. H. Simonds Co., Boston.

- [vii]-viii, 1l., [3]-227p., 8 pl. done in green, orange, black, blue and red incl. front., 17x11cm.

- tan cloth on bds.; illus. stamped in black, green & red; lettering stamped in black and bordered in black.

- "To all little children and to all those crowned with the glory of many years who still retain that priceless possession, the heart of a child, this little volume is affectionately dedicated."

- I.   When Mr. Bluebird Won His Beautiful Coat [*PHJ* (May 1916), 34]
II.   When Old Mr. Gopher First Got Pockets [*PHJ* (Sept. 1916), 34]
III.   When Old Mr. Grouse Got His Snowshoes [*PHJ* (Feb. 1915), 34]
IV.   When Old Mr. Panther Lost His Honor [*PHJ* (Mar. 1916), 38]
V.   When Old Mr. Rat Became an Outcast [*PHJ* (Dec. 1915), 38]
VI.   When Mr. Moose Lost His Horns [*PHJ* (Jan. 1916), 30]
VII.   When Mr. Kingfisher Took to the Ground [*PHJ* (Oct. 1916), 42]
VIII.   When Old Mr. Badger Learned to Stay at Home [*PHJ* (Apr. 1916), 38]
IX.   When Bob White Won His Name [*PHJ* (Jan. 1917), 30]
X.   When Teeny-Weeny Became Grateful [*PHJ* (Feb. 1917), 38]
XI.   When Old Mr. Hare Became a Turncoat [*PHJ* (June 1916), 30]
XII.   When Great-Grandfather Swift First Used a Chimney [*PHJ* (Nov. 1916), 34]
XIII.   When Peter Rabbit First Met Bluffer the Adder [*PHJ* (Aug. 1916), 4]
XIV.   When Mr. Wood Mouse Learned From the Birds [*PHJ* (Dec. 1916), 38]

XV.   When Mr. Hummingbird Got His Long Bill [*PHJ* (Mar. 1917), 38]
XVI.   When Old Mr. Bat Got His Wings [*BtS* (Aug. 21, 1912)]

B.   BURGESS TRADE QUADDIES MARK / [rule] / MOTHER WEST WIND /
"WHEN" STORIES / BY / THORNTON W. BURGESS / Illustrations by /
HARRISON CADY / GROSSET & DUNLAP / PUBLISHERS   NEW YORK
/ By arrangement with Little, Brown, and Company

• c.1917 [1st pub. by G&D in 1941].

• Same collation as 7A except only 4 b&w pl. incl. front.

• Same binding as 7A except for green cloth on bds., and illus. stamped in black
  & blue, d.w. with full-col. illus., end papers #1.

• Same dedication and contents as 7A.

8.   MOTHER WEST WIND
"WHERE" STORIES — 1918

A.   BURGESS TRADE QUADDIES MARK / [rule] / MOTHER WEST WIND /
"WHERE" STORIES / BY / THORNTON W. BURGESS / Author of "Old
Mother West Wind," / "The Bed Time Story-Books," etc. / Illustrations in
Color by / HARRISON CADY / [pub. logo] / BOSTON / LITTLE, BROWN,
AND COMPANY / 1918

• c.1918.

• [v]-vi, 1l., [3]-244p., 8 pl. done in green, orange, & black incl. front., 17x11cm.

• tan cloth on bds.; illus. stamped in black, green & red; lettering stamped in black
  and bordered in black.

•   I.   Where Grandfather Frog Got His Big Mouth [*PHJ* (Sept. 1917), 4]
    II.   Where Miser the Trade Rat First Set Up Shop [*PHJ* (June 1917), 30]
    III.   Where Yap-Yap the Prairie Dog First Used His Wits [*PHJ* (Oct. 1917), 42]
    IV.   Where Yellow-Wing Got His Liking For the Ground [*PHJ* (Aug. 1917), 4]
    V.   Where Little Chief Learned to Make Hay [*PHJ* (Apr. 1917), 4]
    VI.   Where Glutton the Wolverine Got His Name [*PHJ* (Apr. 1918), 34]
    VII.   Where Old Mrs. 'Gator Made the First Incubator [*PHJ* (May 1917), 34]
    VIII. Where Mr. Quack Got His Webbed Feet [*PHJ* (July 1917)]
    IX.   Where Thunderfoot the Bison Got His Hump [*PHJ* (Mar. 1918), 38]
    X.   Where Limberheels Got His Long Tail [*PHJ* (Feb. 1918), 38]
    XI.   Where Old Mr. Gobbler Got the Strutting Habit [*PHJ* (Nov. 1917), 4]
    XII.   Where Seek-Seek Got His Pretty Coat [*PHJ* (Dec. 1917), 38]
    XIII. Where Old Mr. Osprey Learned to Fish [*PHJ* (Jul. 1916), 26]
    XIV.   Where Old Mr. Bob-Cat Left His Honor [*PHJ* (Jan. 1918), 4]
    XV.   Where Dippy the Loon Got the Name of Being Crazy [*PHJ* (May 1918), 38]
    XVI.   Where Big-Horn Got His Curved Horns [*PHJ* (June 1918), 30]

B.   BURGESS <u>TRADE</u> QUADDIES <u>MARK</u> / [rule] / MOTHER WEST WIND /
"WHERE" STORIES / BY / THORNTON W. BURGESS / Illustrations by /
HARRISON CADY / GROSSET & DUNLAP / PUBLISHERS   NEW YORK
/ By arrangement with Little, Brown, and Company

- c.1918 [1st pub. by G&D in 1941].
- Same collation as 8A except only 4 b&w pl. incl. front.
- Same binding as 8A except green cloth on bds., illus. stamped in black and blue, d.w. with full-col. illus., end papers #1.
- Same contents as 8A.

Two later books were collections of stories from the Mother West Wind Series:

Why Peter Rabbit's Ears are Long and Three Other Stories, see page 124.
Mother West Wind Stories to Read Aloud, see page 102.

Cover of *The Boy Scouts of Woodcraft Camp*. Philadelphia, Penn Pub. Co., c.1912. Illus. by C.S. Corson. This printing has a cover illus. from a plate in *The Boy Scouts on Swift River*.

BOY SCOUT SERIES (1912-1915)

The Boy Scouts of America was formed about the same time Burgess began writing his books. Several fiction stories were written for boys on scouting, and Burgess himself created his own Boy Scout Series. His books were submitted to the Boy Scout headquarters for approval and suggestions. After one story was submitted by the publishers, Burgess received

> a kindly letter, saying that the only change they would suggest concerned an incident wherein a troop of Boy Scouts went to the aid of a New York policeman at the time of a street accident and . . . formed a circle around the injured man, thus holding back the crowd.*

The Boy Scout officials suggested that

> it was not best to have boys in fiction do things in fiction that boys in real life could not do.*

Burgess cut out that incident, but

> even before the proofs had been read, occurred the famous suffragette parade in Washington [1913], at which Boy Scouts put the police to shame by . . . holding back a turbulent crowd when police failed to do so.*

This incident strengthened Burgess's faith in the Boy Scout movement.

A theme in the books is that the Boy Scout way is the best way. Tenderfeet are greatly improved after their Boy Scout experiences. Boys who do things their own way fail, but succeed when they adopt proper Scout procedures. A healthy combination of book learning and practical experience is emphasized.

Reprintings of the books of the series brought a few minor changes. The titles of all four books were added to the title page, the introduction, the end of the text, and a biographical sketch of Burgess. Cover illustrations were sometimes exchanged with pictures from other volumes (e.g. front. from *Boy Scouts on Swift River* was used as the cover illus. for *Boy Scouts of Woodcraft Camp*). The title page dates were changed with later printings, and the white

*Thornton W. Burgess, "Making Men of Them," *Good Housekeeping,* 59 (July 1914), 8.

spine lettering was changed to black. The fine wood grain pattern of the end papers was changed to a coarser pattern.

The four Boy Scout books are:
1. The Boy Scouts of Woodcraft Camp - 1912
2. The Boy Scouts on Swift River - 1913
3. The Boy Scouts on Lost Trail - 1914
4. The Boy Scouts in a Trapper's Camp - 1915

1.   THE BOY SCOUTS OF WOODCRAFT CAMP — 1912

The Boy Scouts / of / Woodcraft Camp / By / Thornton W. Burgess / [Boy Scout symbol] / Illustrated by C. S. Corson / The Penn Publishing / Company Philadelphia

- c.1912.

- [4]-345p., 7 illus. (5 b&w pl. incl. front., 2 line diagrams), 19x12 cm.

- brown cloths on bds.; lettering stamped in black, black border; pasted illus. in green, orange, & black; lettering on spine stamped in white; end papers done in wood grain pattern; white d.w. with illus. done in 3 col., green lettering and gold Boy Scout emblem on spine.

- The twofold purpose of the book is ''to stimulate on the part of every one of my boy readers a desire to master for himself the mysteries of nature's great out-of-doors, the secrets of field and wood and stream, and to show by example what the Boy Scout's oath means in the development of character. Many of the incidents . . . are drawn from my own experiences.''

- ''To my wife.''

- XX Chapters. Walter Upton, a Boy Scout from New York City, makes new friends and learns many of nature's ways during his summer's stay at Woodcraft Camp. The story is set in New York's Adirondack Mountains.

2.   THE BOY SCOUTS ON SWIFT RIVER — 1913

The Boy Scouts / on / Swift River / By / Thornton W. Burgess / Author of / The Boy Scouts of Woodcraft Camp / [Boy Scout symbol] / Illustrated by C. S. Corson / The Penn Publishing / Company   Philadelphia / 1913

- c.1913.

- [4]-336p., 8 b&w pl. incl. front., 19x12cm.

- brown cloth on bds.; lettering stamped in black, black border; pasted illus. in green, orange, & black; lettering on spine stamped in white; end papers done in wood grain pattern; white d.w. with illus. done in 3 col., green lettering and gold Boy Scout emblem on spine.

- "To the Boy Scouts."

- XX Chapters. The story is set in the Adirondack Mountains, where the boys use the skills learned at Woodcraft Camp during a canoe trip. One episode about a moose actually happened to the author. Burgess told how he changed one episode in the book in an article, "Making Men of Them," *Good Housekeeping*, 59 (July, 1914), 2-8. (See introduction to the Boy Scout Series in this bibliography, p. 33.)

3.   THE BOY SCOUTS ON LOST TRAIL — 1914

The Boy Scouts / on / Lost Trail / By / Thornton W. Burgess / Author of / The Boy Scouts of Woodcraft Camp / The Boy Scouts on Swift River / [Boy Scout symbol] / Illustrated by C. S. Corson / The Penn Publishing / Company Philadelphia / 1914

- c.1914 Manufacturing Plant, Camden, N.J.

- [4]-362p., 5 b&w pl. incl. front., 19x12cm.

- brown cloth on bds.; lettering stamped in black, black border; pasted illus. in green, orange, & black; lettering on spine stamped in white; end papers done in wood grain pattern; white d.w. with illus. done in 3 col., green lettering and gold Boy Scout emblem on spine.

- "To Franklin K. Mathiews, Chief Librarian of the Boy Scouts of America."

- XX Chapters. The boys' knowledge of woodcraft and self-reliance are put to a more difficult test as they travel to the end of an old Indian trail near Lake Champlain, N.Y.

4.   THE BOY SCOUTS IN
A TRAPPER'S CAMP — 1915

The Boy Scouts / in / A Trapper's Camp / By / Thornton W. Burgess / Author of / "The Boy Scouts of Woodcraft Camp" / "The Boy Scouts on Swift River" / "The Boy Scouts on Lost Trail" / [Boy Scout symbol] / Illustrated by F. A. Anderson / The Penn Publishing / Company   Philadelphia / 1915

- c.1915.

- [4]-362p., 5 b&w pl. incl. front., 19x12cm.

- brown cloth on bds.; lettering stamped in black, black border; pasted illus. in green, orange, & black; lettering on spine stamped in white; end papers done in wood grain pattern; white d.w. with illus. done in 3 col., green lettering and red Boy Scout emblem on spine.

- "To W.H.T., a lover of the open, and his three boys . . ."

- XX Chapters. Their knowledge of scout lore becomes useful when the Scouts spend a winter vacation in the forest.

Covers and title pages of various editions of *The Adventures of Reddy Fox*, the first of Burgess's Bedtime Story-Books

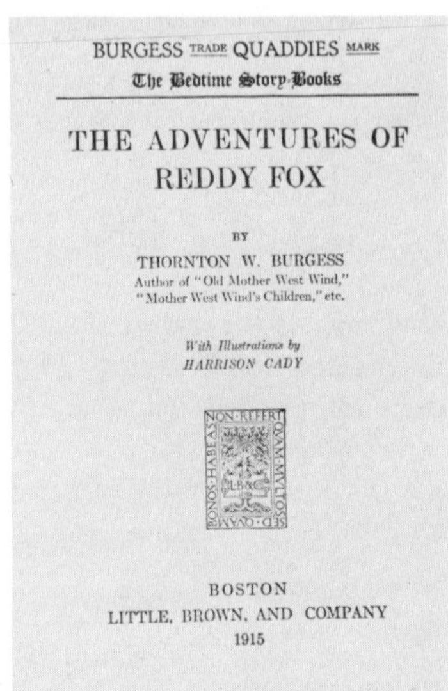

First Edition — 1913. Little, Brown, c.1913. Illus by Harrison Cady. (Right) In the fall of 1915, the Burgess Quaddies trademark first appeared on a just-published Burgess book. It was added to reprintings of already published members of the Mother West Wind Series and The Bedtime Story-Books. This 1915 title page from *The Adventures of Reddy Fox* has the trademark.

BURGESS TRADE QUADDIES MARK
The Bedtime Story-Books

THE ADVENTURES OF
REDDY FOX

BY
THORNTON W. BURGESS
Author of "Old Mother West Wind,"
"Mother West Wind's Children," etc.

McCLELLAND & STEWART, LIMITED
Publishers   Toronto

Title page and dust wrapper of a Canadian version of *The Adventures of Reddy Fox*. They are the same as those of the Little, Brown edition except that the original publisher's name has been replaced by McClelland & Stewart.

THE BEDTIME STORY-BOOKS (1913-1918)

In September 1913 *The Adventures of Reddy Fox* and *The Adventures of Johnny Chuck* were published and became the first two of Burgess's twenty Bedtime Story-Books. They were also the first books to be illustrated by Harrison Cady. The texts of all the books first appeared in Burgess's Bedtime Stories column for the *New York Globe* syndicate (see appendix).

The twenty books are each "The Adventures of . . . " a Green Forest or Green Meadows character. The style and structure of the stories are approximately the same. Most of them are divided into two or three mini-plots. The first few chapters make up the first adventure, which is practically a separate

Color Edition — 1941. Little, Brown, c.1913, renewed 1941 by Thornton W. Burgess. This title page is from a 1944 printing.

story in itself. In *The Adventures of Peter Cottontail,* the first three chapters tell how Peter Rabbit changed his name. Then the books launch into the second plot, which is generally longer and composed of related adventures. In *The Adventures of Peter Cottontail,* Reddy Fox tries many ways to lure Peter from the Dear Old Briar Patch. Sometimes there is a third, short plot, such as the one in which Peter tries to hibernate. The traditional Burgess animal characters and settings appear in each of the books. The point of view in each book is that of the main character, and the reader empathizes with him whether he be Reddy Fox or Poor Mrs. Quack.

In April 1915 Burgess wrote a series of stories for the newspaper about how Peter Rabbit started a quaddy club for his four-footed friends. After this, new volumes of the Bedtime Story-Books were issued under the Burgess Quaddies trademark, beginning with *The Adventures of Chatterer the Red Squirrel* in September 1915. New members of the series and reprintings of the previous eight all had the trademark on the title page.

Little, Brown editions of the series had the words "The Bedtime Story-Books" printed in Old English print on the title page (represented in this bibliography by regular print). The title page dates were changed to correspond with the year of each reprinting. The books each had six b&w pl., and at some point were issued with white dust wrappers with a full-color illustration based on one of the plates. (Also noted is a dust wrapper, perhaps the earliest, with the illus. done in black and red.) Little, Brown also reissued eight members of the series with full-color illustrations in 1941 and 1944.

When Grosset & Dunlap brought out the series from 1949 to 1957, the six illustrations were redrawn, eight more created, and all printed as full-page illustrations in with the regular text, not as plates. The print was done in "large, easy-to-read type." There is one pagination system in each book which changes from Roman to Arabic numerals when the text begins at page 11. The dust wrappers were no longer white but a different color for each member of the series. The covers were brown paper on boards (with a few varieties noted of reddish brown, tan, and green.) End papers were of two types (#2 and mostly #3 in black).

About 1962, Grosset issued the complete series with covers of pink paper on boards, with no dust wrappers. The original d.w. illus. became the cover illus. In 1977 the series came out in tan library binding.

At the end of each Bedtime Story-Book, Burgess told what the next book in the series would be. Grosset numbered the books, but in a different order from that in which they were originally published, so that a person reading one will not find the next book in numerical order to be the same one listed at the end of the previous book. Grosset put the books in alphabetical order except for the last four, which are the last four in chronological order of publication.

This bibliography lists the books in the order they were first published by Little, Brown and Company.

Chronological Order

1. The Adventures of Reddy Fox — 1913
2. The Adventures of Johnny Chuck — 1913
3. The Adventures of Peter Cottontail — 1914
4. The Adventures of Unc' Billy Possum — 1914
5. The Adventures of Mr. Mocker — 1914
6. The Adventures of Jerry Muskrat — 1914
7. The Adventures of Danny Meadow Mouse — 1915
8. The Adventures of Grandfather Frog — 1915
9. The Adventures of Chatterer the Red Squirrel — 1915
10. The Adventures of Sammy Jay — 1915
11. The Adventures of Buster Bear — 1916
12. The Adventures of Old Mr. Toad — 1916
13. The Adventures of Prickly Porky — 1916
14. The Adventures of Old Man Coyote — 1916
15. The Adventures of Paddy the Beaver — 1917
16. The Adventures of Poor Mrs. Quack — 1917
17. The Adventures of Bobby Coon — 1918
18. The Adventures of Jimmy Skunk — 1918
19. The Adventures of Bob White — 1919
20. The Adventures of Ol' Mistah Buzzard — 1919

Grosset & Dunlap Order

The Adventures of . . .

1. Buster Bear
2. Chatterer the Red Squirrel
3. Danny Meadow Mouse
4. Grandfather Frog
5. Jerry Muskrat
6. Johnny Chuck
7. Mr. Mocker
8. Old Man Coyote
9. Old Mr. Toad
10. Paddy the Beaver
11. Peter Cottontail
12. Poor Mrs. Quack
13. Prickly Porky
14. Reddy Fox
15. Sammy Jay
16. Unc' Billy Possum
17. Bobby Coon
18. Jimmy Skunk
19. Bob White
20. Ol' Mistah Buzzard
1 to 20.   Bedtime Stories

1.   THE ADVENTURES OF REDDY FOX — 1913

A.   The Bedtime Story-Books / [rule] / THE ADVENTURES OF / REDDY FOX / BY / THORNTON W. BURGESS / Author of ''Old Mother West Wind,'' / ''Mother West Wind's Children,'' etc. / With Illustrations by / HARRISON CADY / BOSTON / LITTLE, BROWN, AND COMPANY / 1913

- c.1913. Pub. Sept. 1913. Printers S. J. Parkhill & Co., Boston.
- [v]-vi, 1l., [1]-120 p., 6 b&w pl. incl. front., 17x11 cm.
- gray cloth on bds., lettering and illus. stamped in black and red, bordered in red.
- XXVI Chapters. Old Granny Fox has her work cut out for her in making sure Reddy Fox doesn't meet a disastrous end.

B.   The Bedtime Story-Books / [rule] / THE ADVENTURES OF / REDDY FOX / BY / THORNTON W. BURGESS / With Illustrations by / HARRISON CADY / [pub. logo] / BOSTON / LITTLE, BROWN AND COMPANY / 1941

- Burgess Trade Quaddies Mark. c.1913, 1941. Designed and produced by Artists and Writers Guild, Inc.
- 4 p.l., 1-94 p., 10 full-page illus. in col. incl. front., 20x16 cm.
- yellow paper on bds. with red stripe at top and bottom and red cloth spine, black and red lettering, full-col. illus., illus. end papers.
- Same contents as 1A.

C.   The Bedtime Story-Books / [rule] / The Adventures of / Reddy Fox / By THORNTON W. BURGESS / Illustrated by HARRISON CADY / [illus.] / PUBLISHERS / Grosset & Dunlap / NEW YORK

- c.1913, 1941. By arrangement with Little, Brown & Co. [1st pub. by G&D in 1949].
- [iv]-viii - [10]-192 p., 14 full-page b&w illus., 19x12cm.
- brown paper on bds., lettering & illus. stamped in black, d.w. with full-col. illus., end papers #3.
- Same contents as 1A.
- In conjunction with the 1977 reprinting in library binding, *The Adventures of Reddy Fox* was issued in paperback edition, tempo books, Grosset & Dunlap, [iv]-viii, 11-192p., yellow paper covers with col. cover illus.

2.   THE ADVENTURES OF
JOHNNY CHUCK — 1913

A.   The Bedtime Story-Books / [rule] / THE ADVENTURES OF / JOHNNY CHUCK / BY / THORNTON W. BURGESS / Author of ''Old Mother West

Wind,'' / ''The Adventures of Reddy Fox,'' etc. / With Illustrations by / HARRISON CADY / BOSTON / LITTLE, BROWN, AND COMPANY / 1913

- c.1913. Pub. Sept. 1913. Printers S. J. Parkhill & Co., Boston.
- [v]-vi, 1l., [1]-120 p., 6 b&w pl. incl. front., 17x11cm.
- gray cloth on bds., lettering and illus. stamped in black and red, bordered in red.
- XXIV Chapters. Becoming dissatisfied, Johnny Chuck leaves home and sets out to see the Great World.

B.   The Bedtime Story-Books / [rule] / THE ADVENTURES OF / JOHNNY CHUCK / BY / THORNTON W. BURGESS / With Illustrations by / HARRISON CADY / BOSTON / LITTLE, BROWN AND COMPANY / 1944

- Burgess Trade Quaddies Mark. c. 1913, 1944. Designed and produced by Artists and Writers Guild, Inc.
- 3 p.l., 1-96p., 8 full-page illus. in col. incl. front., 20x16cm.
- yellow paper on bds. with red stripe at top and bottom and red cloth spine, black and red lettering, full-col. illus., illus. end papers.
- Same contents as 2A.

C.   The Bedtime Story-Books / [rule] / The Adventures of / Johnny Chuck / By THORNTON W. BURGESS / Illustrated by HARRISON CADY / [illus.] / PUBLISHERS / Grosset & Dunlap / NEW YORK

- c.1913, 1941. By arrangement with Little, Brown & Co. [1st pub. by G&D in 1952].
- [iv]-viii-[10]-191p., 14 full-page b&w illus., 19x12cm.
- brown paper on bds., lettering and illus. stamped in black, d.w. with full-col. illus., end papers #3.
- Same contents as 2A.
- In conjunction with the 1977 reprinting in library binding, *The Adventures of Johnny Chuck* was issued in paperback edition, tempo books, Grosset & Dunlap, [iv]-viii, 11-191p., yellow paper covers with col. cover illus.

3.   THE ADVENTURES OF
PETER COTTONTAIL — 1914

A.   The Bedtime Story-Books / [rule] / THE ADVENTURES OF / PETER COTTONTAIL / BY / THORNTON W. BURGESS / Author of ''The Adventures of Reddy Fox,'' / ''Old Mother West Wind,'' etc. / With Illustrations by / HARRISON CADY / BOSTON / LITTLE, BROWN, AND COMPANY / 1914

- c.1914. Pub. Feb. 1914. Printers S. J. Parkhill & Co., Boston.

- [v]-vi, 1l., [1]-120p., 6 b&w pl. incl. front., 17x11cm.

- gray cloth on bds., lettering and illus. stamped in black and red, bordered in red.

- XXVI Chapters. Peter Rabbit decides to answer only to the name Peter Cottontail. Reddy Fox tries every trick he knows to catch Peter.

B.   The Bedtime Story-Books / [rule] / THE ADVENTURES OF / PETER COTTONTAIL / BY / THORNTON W. BURGESS / With Illustrations by / HARRISON CADY / [pub. logo] / BOSTON / LITTLE, BROWN AND COMPANY / 1941

- Burgess Trade Quaddies Mark. c.1914, 1941. Designed and produced by Artists and Writers Guild Inc.

- 4 p.l., 1-94p., 10 full-page illus. in col. incl. front., 20x16cm.

- yellow paper on bds. with red stripe at top and bottom and red cloth spine, black and red lettering, full-col. illus., illus. end papers.

- Same contents as 3A.

C.   The Bedtime Story-Books / [rule] / The Adventures of / Peter Cottontail / By THORNTON W. BURGESS / Illustrated by HARRISON CADY / [illus.] / PUBLISHERS / Grosset & Dunlap / NEW YORK

- c.1914, 1941. By arrangement with Little, Brown and Company [1st pub. by G&D in 1950].

- [iv]-viii-[10]-192p., 14 full-page b&w illus., 19x12cm.

- brown paper on bds., lettering and illus. stamped in black, d.w. with full-col. illus., end papers #3.

- Same contents as 3A.

- In conjunction with the 1977 reprinting in library binding, *The Adventures of Peter Cottontail* was issued in paperback edition, tempo books, Grosset & Dunlap, 5 p.l., 11-192, yellow paper covers with col. cover illus.

D.   [*The Adventures of Peter Cottontail*, Abridged Edition, has the title page information on a two-page spread. The words "Peter Cottontail" are in large script. The title extends from the verso to the facing recto, causing the print to be set up in the following manner:]

[Verso]   The Adventures of / Peter
[Recto]   By THORNTON W. BURGESS / Illustrated by PHOEBE ERICKSON / Cottontail / Abridged / GROSSET & DUNLAP • NEW YORK

- c.1914 by Little, Brown & Co., c.1941 by T.W. Burgess, c.1958 by Grosset & Dunlap, Inc. [Pub. by G&D in 1958].

- [6]-69p., many full-col. and b&w illus., 32cm.

- yellow paper on bds., green lettering and illus. design, d.w. with full-col. illus.

- Chapters I-XV, XVII of 3A in abridged form.
- This edition came out in a shortened version, pub. by G&D in 1967. [6]-41p., 2 l., 27x20cm., cloth on bds. cover with full-col. illus. same as d.w. of 1958 version. Contents is chapters I-X of 3A in abridged form.

4.   THE ADVENTURES OF
UNC' BILLY POSSUM — 1914

A.   The Bedtime Story Books / [rule] / THE ADVENTURES OF / UNC' BIL-LY POSSUM / BY / THORNTON W. BURGESS / Author of "The Adventures of Peter Cottontail," / "Old Mother West Wind," etc. / With Illustrations by / HARRISON CADY / BOSTON / LITTLE, BROWN, AND COMPANY / 1914

- c.1914. Published February, 1914. Printers S. J. Parkhill & Co., Boston.
- [v]-vi, 1l., [1]-117p., 6 b&w pl. incl. front., 17x11cm.
- gray cloth on bds., lettering and illus. stamped in black and red, bordered in red.
- XXV Chapters. Unc' Billy Possum's troubles start when he steals eggs from Farmer Brown's henhouse.

B.   The Bedtime Story-Books / [rule] / The Adventures of / Unc' Billy Possum / By THORNTON W. BURGESS / Illustrated by HARRISON CADY / [illus.] / PUBLISHERS / Grosset & Dunlap / NEW YORK

- c.1914, 1942. By arrangement with Little, Brown & Co. [1st pub. by G&D in 1951].
- [iv]-viii-[10]-192 p., 14 full-page b&w illus., 19x12cm.
- brown paper on bds., lettering & illus. stamped in black, d.w. with full-col. illus., end papers #3.
- Same contents as 4A.

5.   THE ADVENTURES OF
MR. MOCKER — 1914

A.   The Bedtime Story-Books / [rule] / THE ADVENTURES OF / MR. MOCKER / BY / THORNTON W. BURGESS / Author of "The Adventures of Reddy Fox," / "Old Mother West Wind," etc. / With Illustrations by / HARRISON CADY / BOSTON / LITTLE, BROWN, AND COMPANY / 1914

- c.1914. Published September 1914. Printers S. J. Parkhill & Co., Boston.
- [v]-vi, 1l., [1]-120p., 6 b&w pl. incl. front., 17x11cm.

- gray cloth on bds., lettering and illus. stamped in black and red, bordered in red.

- XXVI Chapters. The Green Forest folk try to solve the mystery of who is making the noises along the Laughing Brook each night.

B.   The Bedtime Story-Books / [rule] / The Adventures of / Mr. Mocker / By THORNTON W. BURGESS / Illustrated by HARRISON CADY / [illus.] / PUBLISHERS / Grosset & Dunlap / NEW YORK

- c.1914, 1942. By arrangement with Little, Brown and Company [1st pub. by G&D in 1951].

- [iv]-viii-[10]-188p., 14 full-page b&w illus., 19x12cm.

- brown paper on bds., lettering and illus. stamped in black, d.w. with full-col. illus., end papers #3.

- Same contents as 5A.

6.   THE ADVENTURES OF
JERRY MUSKRAT — 1914

A.   The Bedtime Story-Books / [rule] / THE ADVENTURES OF / JERRY MUSKRAT / BY / THORNTON W. BURGESS / Author of "The Adventures of Reddy Fox," / "Old Mother West Wind," etc. / With Illustrations by / HARRISON CADY / BOSTON / LITTLE, BROWN, AND COMPANY / 1914

- c.1914. Pub. Sept. 1914. Printers S. J. Parkhill & Co., Boston.

- [v]-vi, 1l., [1]-120p., 6 b&w pl. incl. front., 17x11cm.

- gray cloth on bds., lettering and illus. stamped in black and red, bordered in red.

- XXV Chapters. Jerry Muskrat and his friends try to find out why the Smiling Pool is shrinking.

B.   The Bedtime Story-Books / [rule] / The Adventures of / Jerry Muskrat / By THORNTON W. BURGESS / Illustrated by HARRISON CADY / [illus.] / PUBLISHERS / Grosset & Dunlap / NEW YORK

- c.1914, 1942. By arrangement with Little, Brown & Company [1st pub. by G&D in 1951].

- [iv]-viii-[10]-179p., 14 full-page b&w illus., 19x12cm.

- brown paper on bds., lettering and illus. stamped in black, d.w. with full-col. illus., end papers #3.

- Same contents as 6A.

7. THE ADVENTURES OF
DANNY MEADOW MOUSE — 1915

A.   The Bedtime Story-Books / [rule] / THE ADVENTURES OF / DANNY MEADOW MOUSE / BY / THORNTON W. BURGESS / Author of ''The Adventures of Reddy Fox,'' / ''Old Mother West Wind,'' etc. / With Illustrations by / HARRISON CADY / BOSTON / LITTLE, BROWN, AND COMPANY / 1915

- c.1915. Pub. Feb. 1915. Printers S. J. Parkhill & Co., Boston.
- [v]-vi, 1l., [1]-119p., 6 b&w pl. incl. front., 17x11cm.
- gray cloth on bds., lettering and illus. stamped in black and red, bordered in red.
- XXV Chapters. Danny Meadow Mouse must keep his wits sharp at all times to stay alive.

B.   The Bedtime Story-Books / [rule] / THE ADVENTURES OF / DANNY MEADOW / MOUSE / BY / THORNTON W. BURGESS / With Illustrations by / HARRISON CADY / BOSTON / LITTLE, BROWN AND COMPANY / 1944

- Burgess Trade Quaddies Mark. c.1915, 1944. Designed and produced by Artists and Writers Guild, Inc.
- 4 p.l., 1-94p., 8 full-page illus. in col. incl. front., 20x16 cm.
- yellow paper on bds. with red stripe at top and bottom and red cloth spine, black and red lettering, full-col. illus., illus. end papers.
- Same contents as 7A.

C.   The Bedtime Story-Books / [rule] / The Adventures of / Danny Meadow Mouse / By THORNTON W. BURGESS / Illustrated by HARRISON CADY / [illus.] / PUBLISHERS / Grosset & Dunlap / NEW YORK

- c.1915, 1944. By arrangement with Little, Brown & Company [1st pub. by G&D in 1950].
- [iv]-viii-[10]-187p., 14 full-page b&w illus., 19x12cm.
- brown paper on bds., lettering and illus. stamped in black, d.w. with full-col. illus., illus. end papers (copy examined had end papers #2, a less common variety).
- Same contents as 7A.

<h1 style="text-align:center">8.   THE ADVENTURES OF
GRANDFATHER FROG — 1915</h1>

A.   The Bedtime Story-Books / [rule] / THE ADVENTURES OF / GRAND-FATHER FROG / BY / THORNTON W. BURGESS / Author of ''The Adventures of Reddy Fox,'' / ''Old Mother West Wind,'' etc. / With Illustrations by / HARRISON CADY / BOSTON / LITTLE, BROWN, AND COMPANY / 1915

- c.1915. Pub. February 1915. Printers S. J. Parkhill & Co., Boston.
- [v]-vi, 1l., [1]-120p., 6 b&w pl. incl. front., 17x11cm.
- gray cloth on bds., lettering and illus. stamped in black and red, bordered in red.
- XXIII Chapters. Usually Wise Grandfather Frog does some foolish things, among them setting out to see the Great World.

B.   The Bedtime Story-Books / [rule] / THE ADVENTURES OF / GRAND-FATHER FROG / BY / THORNTON W. BURGESS / With Illustrations by / HARRISON CADY / BOSTON / LITTLE, BROWN AND COMPANY / 1944

- Burgess Trade Quaddies Mark. c.1915, 1944. Designed and produced by Artists and Writers Guild, Inc.
- 4 p.l., 1-96p., 8 full-page illus. in col. incl. front., 20x16cm.
- yellow paper on bds. with red stripe at top and bottom and red cloth spine, black and red lettering, full-col. illus., illus. end papers.
- Same contents as 8A.

C.   The Bedtime Story-Books / [rule] / The Adventures of / Grandfather Frog / By THORNTON W. BURGESS / Illustrated by HARRISON CADY / [illus.] / PUBLISHERS / Grosset & Dunlap / NEW YORK

- c.1915, 1943. By arrangement with Little, Brown & Company [1st pub. by G&D in 1952].
- [iv]-viii-[10]-192p., 14 full-page b&w illus., 19x12cm.
- brown paper on bds., lettering and illus. stamped in black, d.w. with full-col. illus., end papers #3.
- Same contents as 8A.

<h1 style="text-align:center">9.   THE ADVENTURES OF CHATTERER
THE RED SQUIRREL — 1915</h1>

A.   BURGESS TRADE QUADDIES MARK / The Bedtime Story-Books / [rule] / THE ADVENTURES OF / CHATTERER THE RED / SQUIRREL / BY / THORNTON W. BURGESS / Author of ''Old Mother West Wind,'' ''The

46

Adventures / of Johnny Chuck," "Mother West Wind / 'Why' Stories," etc. / With Illustrations by / HARRISON CADY / [pub. logo] / BOSTON / LIT-TLE, BROWN, AND COMPANY / 1915

- c.1915. Published September 1915. The Colonial Press, C. H. Simonds Co., Boston.
- [v]-vi, 1l., [1]-120p., 6 b&w pl. incl. front., 17x11cm.
- gray cloth on bds., lettering and illus. stamped in black and red, bordered in red.
- XXIII Chapters. Chatterer's sharp tongue gets him in trouble with Shadow the Weasel, and his curiosity gets him in trouble with Farmer Brown's Boy.

B.   The Bedtime Story-Books / [rule] / The Adventures of / Chatterer the Red Squirrel / By THORNTON W. BURGESS / Illustrated by HARRISON CADY / [illus.] / PUBLISHERS / Grosset & Dunlap / NEW YORK

- c.1915, 1943. By arrangement with Little, Brown & Company [1st pub. by G&D in 1949].
- [iv]-viii-[10]-190p., 14 full-page b&w illus., 19x12cm.
- brown paper on bds., lettering and illus. stamped in black, d.w. with full-col. illus., end papers #3.
- Same contents as 9A.

10.   THE ADVENTURES OF SAMMY JAY — 1915

A.   BURGESS TRADE QUADDIES MARK / The Bedtime Story-Books / [rule] / THE ADVENTURES OF / SAMMY JAY / BY / THORNTON W. BURGESS / Author of "Old Mother West Wind," "Mother West / Wind 'Why' Stories," "Adventures / of Mr. Mocker," etc. / With Illustrations by / HARRISON CADY / [pub. logo] / BOSTON / LITTLE, BROWN, AND COM-PANY / 1915

- c.1915. Pub. Sept. 1915. The Colonial Press, C. H. Simonds Co., Boston.
- [v]-vi, 1l., [1]-119p., 6 b&w pl. incl. front., 17x11cm.
- gray cloth on bds., lettering and illus. stamped in black and red, bordered in red.
- XXIV Chapters. Sammy Jay carries on his feud with Chatterer the Red Squirrel.

B.   The Bedtime Story-Books / [rule] / The Adventures of / Sammy Jay / By THORNTON W. BURGESS / Illustrated by HARRISON CADY / [illus.] / PUBLISHERS / Grosset & Dunlap / NEW YORK

- c.1915, 1943. By arrangement with Little, Brown & Company [1st pub. by G&D in 1949].
- [iv]-viii-[10]-191p., 14 full-page b&w illus., 19x12cm.
- brown paper on bds., lettering and illus. stamped in black, d.w. with full-col. illus., end papers #3.

- Same contents as 10A.

- In conjunction with the 1977 reprinting in library binding, *The Adventures of Sammy Jay* was issued in paperback edition, tempo books, Grosset & Dunlap, [iv]-viii, 11-191p., yellow paper covers with col. cover illus.

11.   THE ADVENTURES OF BUSTER BEAR — 1916

A.   BURGESS TRADE QUADDIES MARK / The Bedtime Story-Books / [rule] / THE ADVENTURES OF / BUSTER BEAR / BY / THORNTON W. BURGESS / Author of "The Adventures of Reddy Fox," "Old Mother / West Wind," "Mother West Wind 'Why' Stories," etc. / With Illustrations by / HARRISON CADY / [pub. logo] / BOSTON / LITTLE, BROWN, AND COMPANY / 1916

- c.1916. Pub. Mar. 1916. Colonial Press, C. H. Simonds & Co., Boston.

- [iv]-vi, 1l., [1]-120 p., 6 b&w pl. incl. front., 17x11cm.

- gray cloth on bds., lettering and illus. stamped in black and red, bordered in red.

- XXIII Chapters. The Green Forest Folk learn that Buster Bear is afraid of one person — Farmer Brown's Boy.

B.   The Bedtime Story-Books / [rule] / THE ADVENTURES OF / BUSTER BEAR / BY / THORNTON W. BURGESS / With Illustrations by / HARRISON CADY / [pub. logo] / BOSTON / LITTLE, BROWN AND COMPANY / 1941

- Burgess Trade Quaddies Mark. c.1916, 1941. Designed and produced by Artists and Writers Guild, Inc.

- 4 p.l., 1-93p., 10 full-page illus. in col. incl. front., 20x16cm.

- yellow paper on bds., with red stripe at top and bottom and red cloth spine, black and red lettering, full-col. illus., illus. end papers.

- Same contents as 11A.

C.   The Bedtime Story-Books / [rule] / The Adventures of / Buster Bear / By THORNTON W. BURGESS / Illustrated by HARRISON CADY / [illus.] / PUBLISHERS / Grosset & Dunlap / NEW YORK

- c.1916, 1941. By arrangement with Little, Brown, and Company [1st pub. by G&D in 1949].

- [iv]-viii-[10]-189 p., 14 full-page b&w illus., 19x12cm.

- brown paper on bds., lettering and illus. stamped in black, d.w. with full-col. illus., end papers #3.

- Same contents as 11A.

12. THE ADVENTURES OF
OLD MR. TOAD — 1916

A. BURGESS TRADE QUADDIES MARK / The Bedtime Story-Books / [rule] / THE ADVENTURES OF / OLD MR. TOAD / BY / THORNTON W. BURGESS / Author of "The Adventures of Reddy Fox," "Old Mother / West Wind," "Mother West Wind 'Why' Stories," etc. / With Illustrations by / HARRISON CADY / [pub. logo] / BOSTON / LITTLE, BROWN, AND COMPANY / 1916

- c.1916. Pub. Mar. 1916. The Colonial Press, C. H. Simonds & Co., Boston.
- [v]-vi., 1l., [1]-120p., 6 b&w pl. incl. front., 17x11cm.
- gray cloth on bds., lettering and illus. stamped in black and red, bordered in red.
- XXIII Chapters. Peter Rabbit discovers there is much to learn about his long-time friend Old Mr. Toad.

B. The Bedtime Story-Books / [rule] / The Adventures of / Old Mr. Toad / By THORNTON W. BURGESS / Illustrated by HARRISON CADY / [illus.] / PUBLISHERS / Grosset & Dunlap / NEW YORK

- c.1916,1944. By arrangement with Little, Brown & Co. [1st pub. by G&D in 1949].
- [iv]-viii-[10]-192p., 14 full-page b&w illus., 19x12cm.
- brown paper on bds., lettering and illus. stamped in black, d.w. with full-col. illus., end papers #3.
- Same contents as 12A.

13. THE ADVENTURES OF
PRICKLY PORKY — 1916

A. BURGESS TRADE QUADDIES MARK / The Bedtime Story-Books / [rule] / THE ADVENTURES OF / PRICKLY PORKY / BY / THORNTON W. BURGESS / Author of "Old Mother West Wind Series," "Mother / West Wind 'How' Stories," "The Bedtime / Story-Books," etc. / With Illustrations by / HARRISON CADY / [pub. logo] / BOSTON / LITTLE, BROWN, AND COMPANY / 1916

- c.1916. Pub. Sept. 1916. Set up and electrotyped by the Vail Ballou Co., Binghamton, N.Y. Presswork by S. J. Parkhill & Co., Boston.
- 4 p.l., [1]-116p., 6 b&w pl. incl. front., 17x11cm.
- gray cloth on bds., lettering and illus. stamped in black and red, bordered in red.
- XXIII Chapters. The Stranger from the North gives the Green Forest folk a scare.

B.   The Bedtime Story-Books / [rule] / The Adventures of / Prickly Porky / By THORNTON W. BURGESS / Illustrated by HARRISON CADY / [illus.] / PUBLISHERS / Grosset & Dunlap / NEW YORK

- c.1916, 1944. By arrangement with Little, Brown & Co. [1st pub. by G&D in 1949].
- [iv]-viii-[10]-192p., 14 full-page b&w illus., 19x12cm.
- brown paper on bds., lettering and illus. stamped in black, d.w. with full-col. illus., end papers #3.
- Same contents as 13A.

14.   THE ADVENTURES OF
OLD MAN COYOTE — 1916

A.   BURGESS TRADE QUADDIES MARK / The Bedtime Story-Books / [rule] / THE ADVENTURES OF / OLD MAN COYOTE / BY / THORNTON W. BURGESS / Author of ''Old Mother West Wind Series,'' ''Mother / West Wind 'How' Stories,'' ''The Bedtime / Story-Books,'' etc. / With Illustrations by / HARRISON CADY / [pub. logo] / BOSTON / LITTLE, BROWN, AND COMPANY / 1916

- c.1916. Pub. Sept. 1916. Set up and electrotyped by Vail Ballou Co., Binghamton, N.Y. Presswork by S. J. Parkhill & Co., Boston, Mass.
- [v]-vi, 1l., [1]-120p., 6 b&w pl. incl. front., 17x11cm.
- gray cloth on bds., lettering and illus. stamped in black and red, bordered in red.
- XXIII Chapters. Old Man Coyote's arrival on the Green Meadows brings fear to the hearts of the meadow folk and anger to Granny and Reddy Fox, since he proves trickier than they.

B.   The Bedtime-Story Books / [rule] / The Adventures of / Old Man Coyote / By THORNTON W. BURGESS / Illustrated by HARRISON CADY / [illus.] / PUBLISHERS / Grosset & Dunlap / NEW YORK

- c.1916, 1944. By arrangement with Little, Brown, and Company [1st pub. by G&D in 1952].
- [iv]-viii-[10]-192p., 14 full-page b&w illus., 19x12cm.
- brown paper on bds., lettering and illus. stamped in black, d.w. with full-col. illus., end papers #3.
- Same contents as 14A.

15.   THE ADVENTURES OF
PADDY THE BEAVER — 1917

A.   BURGESS <u>TRADE</u> QUADDIES <u>MARK</u> / The Bedtime Story-Books / [rule] /
THE ADVENTURES OF / PADDY THE BEAVER / BY / THORNTON W.
BURGESS / Author of "Old Mother West Wind," "The Bedtime / Story-
Books," etc. / With Illustrations by / HARRISON CADY / [pub. logo] /
BOSTON / LITTLE, BROWN, AND COMPANY / 1917

- c.1917. Pub. Mar. 1917. Printers S. J. Parkhill & Co., Boston.
- [v]-vi, 1l., [1]-118p., 6 b&w pl. incl. front., 17x11cm.
- gray cloth on bds., lettering and illus. stamped in black and red, bordered in red.
- XXII Chapters. Being a hard worker, Paddy the Beaver builds a dam in the Green Forest.

B.   The Bedtime Story-Books / [rule] / The Adventures of / Paddy the Beaver
/ By THORNTON W. BURGESS / Illustrated by HARRISON CADY / [illus.]
/ PUBLISHERS / Grosset & Dunlap / NEW YORK

- c.1917,1945. By arrangement with Little, Brown, and Company [1st pub. by G&D in 1951].
- [iv]-viii-[10]-180p., 14 full-page b&w illus., 19x12cm.
- brown paper on bds., lettering and illus. stamped in black, d.w. with full-col. illus., end papers #3.
- Same contents as 15A.

16.   THE ADVENTURES OF
POOR MRS. QUACK — 1917

A.   BURGESS <u>TRADE</u> QUADDIES <u>MARK</u> / The Bedtime Story-Books / [rule] /
THE ADVENTURES OF / POOR MRS. QUACK / BY / THORNTON W.
BURGESS / Author of "Old Mother West Wind," "The Bedtime / Story-
Books," etc. / With Illustrations by / HARRISON CADY / [pub. logo] /
BOSTON / LITTLE, BROWN, AND COMPANY / 1917

- c.1917. Pub. Mar. 1917. Printers S. J. Parkhill & Co., Boston.
- [v]-vi, 1l., [1]-119p., 6 b&w pl. incl. front., 17x11cm.
- gray cloth on bds., lettering and illus. stamped in black and red, bordered in red.
- XX Chapters. The Green Meadow folk join Mrs. Quack in a search for her lost hus-band. The cruelty and harshness of duck hunting is shown using the duck's point of view.

- Dr. William T. Hornaday, director of the New York Zoological Park, asked Burgess to aid "in the bitter fight to save . . . the once vast duck population." [Burgess said that] "Immediately I started in my syndicated column a series of stories portraying the life of Mrs. Quack the Mallard Duck. . . . I tried to make clear the utterly heartless treachery of baiting waters, and the use of live decoys."* The book did not endear Burgess to duck hunters.† The stories ran in the syndicated column from Mar. to May 1916.

B.   The Bedtime Story-Books / [rule] / The Adventures of / Poor Mrs. Quack / By THORNTON W. BURGESS / Illustrated by HARRISON CADY / [illus.] / PUBLISHERS / Grosset & Dunlap / NEW YORK

- c.1917,1945. By arrangement with Little, Brown & Company [1st pub. by G&D in 1953].

- [iv]-viii-[10]-189p., 14 full-page b&w illus., 19x12cm.

- brown paper on bds., lettering and illus. stamped in black, d.w. with full-col. illus., end papers #3.

- Same contents as 16A.

17.   THE ADVENTURES OF BOBBY COON — 1918

A.   BURGESS TRADE QUADDIES MARK / The Bedtime Story-Books / [rule] / THE ADVENTURES OF / BOBBY COON / BY / THORNTON W. BURGESS / Author of "Old Mother West Wind," / "The Bedtime Story-Books," etc. / With Illustrations by / HARRISON CADY / [pub. logo] / BOSTON / LITTLE, BROWN, AND COMPANY / 1918

- c.1918. Pub. Apr. 1918.

- 4 p.l., [1]-117p., 6 b&w pl. incl. front., 17x11cm.

- gray cloth on bds., lettering and illus. stamped in black and red bordered in red.

- XXIII Chapters. After Farmer Brown's Boy cuts down Bobby Coon's tree with Bobby inside, the raccoon finds himself with a broken leg and no home.

B.   The Bedtime Story-Books / [rule] / THE ADVENTURES OF / BOBBY COON / BY / THORNTON W. BURGESS / With Illustrations by / HARRISON CADY / BOSTON / LITTLE, BROWN AND COMPANY / 1944

- Burgess Trade Quaddies Mark. c.1918, 1944. Designed and produced by Artists and Writers Guild, Inc.

- 5 p.l., 1-94p., 8 full-page illus. in col. incl. front., 20x16cm.

---

*Thornton W. Burgess, *Now I Remember* (Boston, Little, Brown, 1960), p. 131.

†Russell A. Lovell, Jr., *The Cape Cod Story of Thornton W. Burgess* (Sandwich, Mass., Thornton W. Burgess Centennial Committee, 1974), p. 68.

- yellow paper on bds. with red stripe at top and bottom and red cloth spine, black and red lettering, full-col. illus., illus. end papers.

- Same contents as 17A.

C.   The Bedtime Story-Books / [rule] / The Adventures of / Bobby Coon / By THORNTON W. BURGESS / Illustrated by HARRISON CADY / [illus.] / PUBLISHERS / Grosset & Dunlap / NEW YORK

- c.1918,1946. By arrangement with Little, Brown & Company [1st pub. by G&D in 1954].

- [iv]-viii-[10]-188p., 14 full-page b&w illus., 19x12cm.

- brown paper on bds., lettering and illus. stamped in black, d.w. with full-col. illus., end papers #3.

- Same contents as 17A.

18.   THE ADVENTURES OF JIMMY SKUNK — 1918

A.   BURGESS TRADE QUADDIES MARK / The Bedtime Story-Books / [rule] / THE ADVENTURES OF / JIMMY SKUNK / BY / THORNTON W. BURGESS / Author of "Old Mother West Wind," / "The Bedtime Story-Books," etc. / With Illustrations by / HARRISON CADY / [pub. logo] / BOSTON / LITTLE, BROWN, AND COMPANY / 1918

- c.1918. Pub. Apr. 1918.

- 4 p.l., [1]-118p., 6 b&w pl. incl. front., 17x11cm.

- gray cloth on bds., lettering and illus. stamped in black and red, bordered in red.

- XXIII Chapters. Jimmy Skunk has special methods of dealing with the tricks of Peter Rabbit, Reddy Fox, and Unc' Billy Possum.

B.   The Bedtime Story-Books / [rule] / THE ADVENTURES OF / JIMMY SKUNK / BY / THORNTON W. BURGESS / With Illustrations by / HARRISON CADY / [pub. logo] / BOSTON / LITTLE, BROWN AND COMPANY / 1941

- Burgess Trade Quaddies Mark . c.1918, 1941. Designed and produced by Artists and Writers Guild, Inc.

- 5 p.l., 1-94p., 10 full-page illus. in col. incl. front., 20x16cm.

- yellow paper on bds. with red stripe at top and bottom and red cloth spine, black and red lettering, full-col. illus., illus. end papers.

- Same contents as 18A.

C.   The Bedtime Story-Books / [rule] / The Adventures of / Jimmy Skunk /
By THORNTON W. BURGESS / Illustrated by HARRISON CADY / [illus.] /
PUBLISHERS / Grosset & Dunlap / NEW YORK

- c.1918, 1946. By arrangement with Little, Brown and Company [1st pub. by G&D in 1955].
- [iv]-viii-[10]-189p., 14 full-page b&w illus., 19x12cm.
- brown paper on bds., lettering and illus. stamped in black, d.w. with full-col. illus., end papers #3.
- Same contents as 18A.

19.   THE ADVENTURES OF BOB WHITE — 1919

A.   BURGESS TRADE QUADDIES MARK / The Bedtime Story-Books / [rule] /
THE ADVENTURES OF / BOB WHITE / BY / THORNTON W. BURGESS /
Author of "Old Mother West Wind," / "The Bedtime Story-Books," etc. /
With Illustrations by / HARRISON CADY / [pub. logo] / BOSTON / LIT-
TLE, BROWN, AND COMPANY / 1919

- c.1919.
- [v]-vi, 1l., [1]-117p., 6 b&w pl. incl. front., 17x11cm.
- gray cloth on bds., lettering and illus. stamped in black and red, bordered in red.
- XXII Chapters. This story tells the struggles of Mr. and Mrs. Bob White in rearing a family.

B.   The Bedtime Story-Books / [rule] / The Adventures of / Bob White / By
THORNTON W. BURGESS / Illustrated by HARRISON CADY / [illus.] /
PUBLISHERS / Grosset & Dunlap / NEW YORK

- c.1919. By arrangement with Little, Brown and Company [1st pub. by G&D in 1956].
- [iv]-viii-[10]-186p., 14 full-page b&w illus., 19x12cm.
- brown paper on bds., lettering and illus. stamped in black, d.w. with full-color illus., end papers #3.
- Same contents as 19A.

20.   THE ADVENTURES OF
OL' MISTAH BUZZARD — 1919

A.   BURGESS TRADE QUADDIES MARK / The Bedtime Story-Books / [rule] /
THE ADVENTURES OF / OL' MISTAH BUZZARD / BY / THORNTON W.
BURGESS / Author of "Old Mother West Wind," / "The Bedtime Story-

Books,'' etc. / With Illustrations by / HARRISON CADY / [pub. logo] / BOSTON / LITTLE, BROWN, AND COMPANY / 1919

- c.1919.
- [v]-vi, 1l., [1]-119p., 6 b&w pl. incl. front., 17x11cm.
- gray cloth on bds., lettering and illus. stamped in black and red, bordered in red.
- XXV Chapters. Peter Rabbit sets out to learn all about Ol' Mistah Buzzard who has just arrived on the Green Meadows. Mistah Buzzard tells the legend of why buzzards don't build nests.

B.   The Bedtime Story-Books / [rule] / The Adventures of / Ol' Mistah Buzzard / By THORNTON W. BURGESS / Illustrated by HARRISON CADY / [illus.] / PUBLISHERS / Grosset & Dunlap / NEW YORK

- c.1919, 1947. By arrangement with Little, Brown and Company [1st pub. by G&D in 1957].
- [iv]-viii-[10]-192p., 14 full-page b&w illus., 19x12cm.
- paper on bds. (green cover on copy examined), lettering and illus. stamped in black, d.w. with full-col. illus., end papers #3.
- Same contents as 20A.

1 to 20.   BEDTIME STORIES — 1959

THORNTON W. BURGESS / Bedtime Stories / Illustrated by CARL and MARY HAUGE / [illus.] / GROSSET & DUNLAP • Publishers • NEW YORK

- c.1959. By arrangement with Little, Brown & Company.
- [6]-103-[105]p., many full-col. and gray & white illus., 31x22cm.
- 2 varieties of bindings: (1) yellow paper on bds. with green cloth spine, green illus. on cover, full-col. d.w., illus. end papers (2) paper on bds. with full-col. illus. same as d.w. illus. of #1, illus. end papers.
- The 20 stories in the book are each an abridgement of an excerpt from the 20 Bedtime Story-Books. They follow the numerical order of the Grosset & Dunlap editions.

Buster Bear Goes Fishing [from Chapters I & II of *The Adventures of Buster Bear*]

Chatterer the Red Squirrel Learns His Lesson [from Ch. I & II of *The Adventures of Chatterer the Red Squirrel*]

Danny Meadow Mouse Wants a New Tail [from Ch. I & II of *The Adventures of Danny Meadow Mouse*]

Grandfather Frog Gets into Trouble [from Ch. VII & VIII of *The Adventures of Grandfather Frog*]

Jerry Muskrat Has a Fright [from Ch. I & IV of *The Adventures of Jerry Muskrat*]

Johnny Chuck Finds the Greatest Thing [from Ch. X & XI of *The Adventures of Johnny Chuck*]

Mr. Mocker Makes New Friends [from Ch. XXV & XXVI of *The Adventures of Mr. Mocker*]

Old Man Coyote Meets a Neighbor [from Ch. VIII & IX of *The Adventures of Old Man Coyote*]

A Discovery About Old Mr. Toad [from Ch. VII & VI of *The Adventures of Old Mr. Toad*]

Paddy the Beaver Wins an Argument [from Ch. IV of *The Adventures of Paddy the Beaver*]

Peter Cottontail Has Two Close Calls [from Ch. XIV, XXIII, & XXVI of *The Adventures of Peter Cottontail*]

Poor Mrs. Quack Finds Happiness [from Ch. VIII & XX of *The Adventures of Poor Mrs. Quack*]

Prickly Porky is a Friend Indeed [from Ch. III & XVIII of *The Adventures of Prickly Porky*]

Reddy Fox Learns a New Trick [from Ch. I & II of *The Adventures of Reddy Fox*]

Sammy Jay Gets Caught [from Ch. I & II of *The Adventures of Sammy Jay*]

Unc' Billy Possum Escapes [from Ch. XXIV & XXV of *The Adventures of Unc' Billy Possum*]

Bobby Coon Meets a Kind Boy [from Ch. VII & VIII of *The Adventures of Bobby Coon*]

Jimmy Skunk Uses His Perfume [from Ch. III & IV of *The Adventures of Jimmy Skunk*]

Bob White Keeps His Home a Secret [from Ch. I, IV, & VIII of *The Adventures of Bob White*]

Why Ol' Mistah Buzzard Doesn't Have a Nest [from Ch. XX, XXI, & XXII of *The Adventures of Ol' Mistah Buzzard*]

- Since the author's name appears at the head of the title, it is also known as *Thornton W. Burgess Bedtime Stories*.

- It was also issued in Grosset's Dandelion Library format, 23cm. (bound back to back with ''The Pony Engine,'' an adaptation of Frances M. Ford's ''The Little Engine That Could''). Also issued in a paper covers version in 1976, (Elephant Books).

Cover of *The Bedtime Story Calendar*. Chicago,
P.F. Volland & Co., c.1915.

THE BEDTIME STORY CALENDAR (1915)

[illus.] / The Bedtime Story / Calendar / Enchanting Tales / of / Field and
Forest Playmates / for / Little People / BY / THORNTON W. BURGESS /
Author of / "Old Mother West Wind Stories," / etc., etc. / [illus.] / [symbol]
/ P. F. VOLLAND & CO., Publishers / New York Chicago Toronto

- c.1915 P. F. Volland & Co., Chicago (from cover).

- 54 l. (t.p. & 53 l. of stories), illus. done in blue and black, 27x14cm.

- paper covers, black and pink lettering, illus. done in blue, pink, green, black &
  yellow, printing parallel to binding, issued in a box, silk cord and tassel tied.

- 53 stories, one per leaf, corresponding to the weeks of the year.

- Volland Book Calendars and Year Books (Although the book gives the copyright date
  as 1915, the Catalogue of Copyright Entries lists it under 1914. The book was ap-
  parently for the calendar year 1915.)

Cover of the 1921 edition of *Tommy and the Wishing-Stone*. Boston, Little, Brown, c.1915, renewed 1943, c.1921, renewed 1949 by Thornton W. Burgess. Illus. by Harrison Cady.

THE WISHING-STONE SERIES (1915)

The three books in the series tell what happens to a boy named Tommy whenever he sits upon a great rock in the Green Meadows. Although it goes unsaid, Tommy is obviously Farmer Brown's Boy of many other Burgess stories. (The first story in *Old Mother West Wind* gives Farmer Brown's Boy's first name as Tommy.) In each story, Tommy becomes one of the Green Meadow or Green Forest folk and learns the joys and difficulties of each of their lives. There is little doubt that each adventure is one of Tommy's daydreams. These experiences change Tommy's character into that of a wild-animal lover. If these stories are read in their chronological place with the Mother West Wind Series and the Bedtime Story-Books, the change in Farmer Brown's Boy's character can be understood. In the early books he is an enemy of the animals and delights in hunting them with his dreadful gun. In the later ones he becomes their friend and tries to learn as much about them as he can.

The stories and the Cady illustrations were originally serialized in *St. Nicholas* magazine from November 1914 to October 1915. The Century Company, publishers of *St. Nicholas* magazine at that time, brought out the book *Tommy and the Wishing Stone* in 1915, with the stories arranged in this book in the same order that they appeared in *St. Nicholas*.

Little, Brown and Company brought out the stories in three volumes in 1921: *Tommy and the Wishing Stone, Tommy's Wishes Come True,* and *Tommy's Change of Heart.* The books, now called The Wishing Stone Series, had the series name printed in Old English print on the title page. The twelve stories, four in each book, were no longer in the original *St. Nicholas* order. In 1935, Little, Brown also brought out the three books in one volume called *The Wishing-Stone Stories.*

When Grosset & Dunlap obtained the rights to the books, they brought out their edition in 1959, once again in three volumes. The series was called The Wishing-Stone Stories. The glossy plates were replaced by Cady line drawings based on the originals and printed on the regular text paper. They also came with illustrated dust wrappers and end papers (#3 in green).

    1-2-3.   Tommy and the Wishing Stone — 1915 (Century Co.)
        1.   Tommy and the Wishing-Stone — 1921 (Little, Brown, G&D)
        2.   Tommy's Wishes Come True — 1921 (Little, Brown, G&D)
        3.   Tommy's Change of Heart — 1921 (Little, Brown, G&D)
    1-2-3.   The Wishing-Stone Stories — 1935 (Little, Brown)

1-2-3. TOMMY AND THE WISHING STONE —
1915   (Century Co.)

TOMMY AND THE / WISHING STONE / BY / THORNTON W. BURGESS / Author of "Old Mother West Wind," "The Adven- / tures of Reddy Fox," etc. / WITH ILLUSTRATIONS BY / HARRISON CADY / [pub. logo] / NEW YORK / THE CENTURY CO. / 1915

- c.1915, Pub. September, 1915.

- [vi]-vii, 1l., [2]-290p., 48 b&w pl. incl. front., 18x12cm.

- tan cloth on bds., bordered in green, title stamped in gold, illus. stamped in red and green.

- "To the cause of love, mercy and protection for our little friends of the air and the wild-wood and to a better understanding of them this little book is dedicated."

- I.   Tommy and the Wishing-Stone [*St. Nicholas*, XLII (Nov. 1914), 59-63.]
  II.   Why Tommy Became a Friend of Red Squirrels [*SN*, XLII (Dec. 1914), 152-156.]
 III.   Why Peter Rabbit Has One Less Enemy [*SN*, XLII (Jan. 1915), 256-260.]
 IV.   How It Happened That Reddy Fox Gained a Friend [*SN*, XLII (Feb. 1915), 351-356.]
  V.   How Tommy Envied Honker the Goose [*SN*, XLII (Mar. 1915), 425-429.]
 VI.   Tommy Becomes a Very Humble Person [*SN*, XLII (Apr. 1915), 542-546.]
 VII.   Why Tommy Took Up All His Traps [*SN*, XLII (May 1915), 638-643.]
VIII.   How Tommy Learned to Admire Thunderer the Ruffed Grouse [*SN*, XLII (June 1915), 718-723.]
 IX.   What Happened When Tommy Became a Mink [*SN*, XLII (July 1915), 815-819.]
  X.   The Pleasures and Troubles of Bobby Coon [*SN*, XLII (Aug. 1915), 934-938.]
 XI.   Tommy Becomes a Furry Engineer [*SN*, XLII (Sept. 1915), 1029-1033.]
 XII.   Tommy Learns What It Is Like To Be a Bear [*SN*, XLII (Oct. 1915), 1116-1120.]

1. TOMMY AND THE WISHING-STONE — 1921
(Little, Brown and G&D)

A. The Wishing-Stone Series / [rule] / TOMMY AND THE / WISHING-

STONE / BY / THORNTON W. BURGESS / WITH ILLUSTRATIONS BY / HARRISON CADY / [pub. logo] / BOSTON / LITTLE, BROWN, AND COMPANY / 1921

- c.1915, 1921.

- 5 p.l., [1]-109p., 8 b&w pl. incl. front., 19x12cm.

- green cloth on bds., paper pasted on cover with full-col. illus. and yellow and black lettering.

- Same dedication as 1-2-3 above, except the words "this little book is dedicated" are changed to "the Wishing-Stone Stories are dedicated."

- I.   Tommy and the Wishing-Stone
  II.   How Tommy Learned to Admire Thunderer the Ruffed Grouse
  III. What Happened When Tommy Became a Mink
  IV. Tommy Becomes a Very Humble Person

B.   THE WISHING-STONE STORIES / [rule] / Tommy and the / Wishing-Stone / By / THORNTON W. BURGESS / ILLUSTRATED BY / HARRISON CADY / [rule] / PUBLISHERS / Grosset & Dunlap / NEW YORK

- c.1915, 1921. By arrangement with Little, Brown and Company [1st pub. by G&D in 1959].

- 4 p.l., [1]-109p., 8 b&w pl. incl. front. (on verso of half-title), 19x12cm.

- blue paper on bds., illus. on cover and lettering on spine stamped in black, d.w. with full-col. illus., end papers #3.

- Same dedication and contents as 1A.

2. TOMMY'S WISHES COME TRUE — 1921
(Little, Brown and G&D)

A.   The Wishing-Stone Series / [rule] / TOMMY'S WISHES / COME TRUE / BY / THORNTON W. BURGESS / WITH ILLUSTRATIONS BY / HARRISON CADY / [pub. logo] / BOSTON / LITTLE, BROWN, AND COMPANY / 1921

- c.1915, 1921.

- 4 p.l., [1]-111p., 8 b&w pl. incl. front., 19x12cm.

- green cloth on bds., paper pasted on cover with full-col. illus. and yellow and black lettering.

- I.   Why Peter Rabbit Has One Less Enemy
  II.   Why Tommy Became a Friend of Red Squirrels
  III. The Pleasures and Troubles of Bobby Coon
  IV. How Tommy Envied Honker the Goose

B.   THE WISHING-STONE STORIES / [rule] / Tommy's Wishes / Come
True / By / THORNTON W. BURGESS / ILLUSTRATED BY / HARRISON
CADY / [rule] / PUBLISHERS / Grosset & Dunlap / NEW YORK

* c.1915, 1921. By arrangement with Little, Brown & Co. [1st pub. by G&D in 1959].

* 4 p.l., [1]-111p., 8 b&w pl. incl. front. (on verso of half-title), 19x12cm.

* tan paper on bds., illus. on cover and lettering on spine stamped in black, d.w. with
  full-col. illus., end papers #3.

* Same contents as 2A.

3.   TOMMY'S CHANGE OF HEART — 1921
(Little, Brown and G&D)

A.   The Wishing Stone Series / [rule] / TOMMY'S CHANGE / OF HEART /
BY / THORNTON W. BURGESS / WITH ILLUSTRATIONS BY / HAR-
RISON CADY / [pub. logo] / BOSTON / LITTLE, BROWN, AND COM-
PANY / 1921

* c.1915, 1921.

* 4 p.l., [1]-115p., 8 b&w pl. incl. front., 19x12cm.

* green cloth on bds., paper pasted on cover with full-col. illus. and yellow and
  black lettering.

* I.   How It Happened That Reddy Fox Gained a Friend
  II.   Tommy Becomes a Furry Engineer
  III. Why Tommy Took Up All His Traps
  IV.   Tommy Learns What It Is Like To Be a Bear

B.   THE WISHING-STONE STORIES / [rule] / Tommy's Change / of Heart
/ By / THORNTON W. BURGESS / ILLUSTRATED BY / HARRISON
CADY / [rule] / PUBLISHERS / Grosset & Dunlap / NEW YORK

* c. 1915, 1921. By arrangement with Little, Brown and Company [1st pub. by G&D
  in 1959].

* 3 p.l., [1]-115p., 7 b&w pl. incl. front. (on verso of half-title), 19x12cm.

* green paper on bds., illus. on cover and lettering on spine stamped in black, d.w.
  with full-col. illus., end papers #3.

* Same contents as 3A.

1-2-3. THE WISHING-STONE STORIES — 1935
(Little, Brown)

THE / WISHING-STONE / STORIES / BY / THORNTON W. BURGESS /
WITH ILLUSTRATIONS BY / HARRISON CADY / [pub. logo] / BOSTON
/ LITTLE, BROWN, AND COMPANY / 1935

- c.1915, 1921.
- [vii]-viii, 1 l., [1]-109, 1 l., [1]-111, 1 l., [1]-115p., 16 b&w pl. incl. front., 19x12cm.
- blue cloth on bds., lettering and illus. stamped in brown.
- This book contains the three books in the Wishing-Stone Series: I. Tommy and the
  Wishing-Stone, II. Tommy's Wishes Come True, III. Tommy's Change of Heart.

Illustration by Harrison Cady from *Tommy and the Wishing-Stone*, used in both The Century Co.
edition, c.1915, and the Little, Brown edition, c.1921.

Cover of *Happy Jack* (Green Meadow Series). Boston, Little, Brown, c.1918, renewed 1946 by Thornton W. Burgess. This cover illus. by Harrison Cady.

GREEN MEADOW SERIES (1918-1920)

This group of four books is like a continuation of the Bedtime Story-Books series — telling the adventures of four more animals, all of whom live on the Green Meadows. The books are similar to the Bedtime Story-Books in both style and plot. The stories first appeared as installments in Burgess's newspaper story column.

The Little, Brown editions contained the Burgess Quaddies trademark, the series name in Old English print, and eight color plates by Harrison Cady.

The Grosset editions have had several changes in binding since first brought out in 1943. The first printings (described in this bibliography) had blue paper on board covers, blue lettering, only four of the original eight plates (still on glossy paper but in b&w), col. d.w.'s with original cover illus., and end papers #1 (light green with border). Changes include a t.p. statement of wartime paper, blue cover paper of different texture, end papers #1 done in darker green (finally the present end papers #3 were used), and the glossy plates redone in line drawings.

About 1962, Grosset brought out the series in new green paper on board covers, with no d.w. — the d.w. illus. now appearing right on the cover. Finally in 1977, the series came out in tan library binding with each title preceded by ''The Adventures of. . . .''

The volumes in the series are:
1. Happy Jack - 1918
2. Mrs. Peter Rabbit - 1919
3. Bowser the Hound - 1920
4. Old Granny Fox - 1920
1-2-3-4.   The Burgess Big Book of Green Meadow Stories - 1932

1. HAPPY JACK — 1918

A. HAPPY JACK / BY / THORNTON W. BURGESS / AUTHOR OF
"OLD MOTHER WEST WIND" / "THE BED TIME STORY BOOKS,"
ETC. / Illustrated in color by / Harrison Cady / [pub. logo] / BOSTON / LIT-
TLE, BROWN, AND COMPANY / 1918

- c.1918. Norwood Press. Set up and electrotyped by J. S. Cushing Co., Norwood,
  Mass.

- [vi]-xi, 1-204p., 8 pl. in orange, green, and black incl. front., 20x14cm.

- green cloth on bds.; lettering and design of trees stamped in yellow and dark green;
  full-col. illus. pasted in center (2 versions of the col. illus. exist — one by Harrison
  Cady, one by George Kerr from *Old Mother West Wind*, col. ed., 1914).

- "To Dr. William T. Hornaday, to whom posterity will owe a debt of gratitude for
  his valiant fight to preserve American wild life, who has been a lifelong champion
  of Happy Jack Squirrel, and to whom the author is deeply indebted for encourage-
  ment and assistance, this book is gratefully dedicated."

- XXXIII Chapters. Happy Jack the Gray Squirrel is aided by his friends Tommy Tit
  the Chickadee and Farmer Brown's Boy in escaping from Shadow the Weasel.

B. HAPPY JACK / BY / THORNTON W. BURGESS / With Illustrations by
/ HARRISON CADY / GROSSET & DUNLAP / Publishers   New York /
Printed by arrangement with Little, Brown, and Company

- c.1918 [1st pub. by G&D in 1943].

- [vii]-xi, 1-204p., 4 b&w pl. incl. front., 19x12cm.

- blue paper on bds.; lettering stamped in dark blue; d.w. with full-col. illus.; end
  papers #1.

- Same dedication and contents as 1A.

- The G&D library binding format of 1977 has cover title *The Adventures of Happy
  Jack*.

2. MRS. PETER RABBIT - 1919

A. BURGESS <u>TRADE</u> QUADDIES <u>MARK</u> / Green Meadow Series / [rule] /
MRS. PETER RABBIT / BY / THORNTON W. BURGESS / With Illustrations
by / HARRISON CADY / [pub. logo] / BOSTON / LITTLE, BROWN, AND
COMPANY / 1919

- c.1919. Pub. Sept. 1919. Norwood Press. Set up and electrotyped by J. S. Cushing
  Co., Norwood, Mass.

- [vii]-viii, 1l., [1]-205p., 8 pl. in orange, green, and black incl. front., 20x14cm.

- green cloth on bds.; lettering and design of trees stamped in yellow and dark green; full-col. illus. pasted in center.

- "To my daughter, whose assistance in the preparation of this volume has been invaluable, it is most affectionately dedicated."

- XXXII Chapters. The story tells how Peter Rabbit met, fought for, and won Little Miss Fuzzytail as his bride.

B.   MRS. PETER RABBIT / BY / THORNTON W. BURGESS / With Illustrations by / HARRISON CADY / GROSSET & DUNLAP / Publishers New York / Printed by arrangement with Little, Brown, and Company

- c.1919 [1st pub. by G&D in 1943].

- [vii]-viii, 1l., [1]-205p., 4 b&w pl. incl. front., 19x12cm.

- blue paper on bds.; lettering stamped in dark blue; d.w. with full-col. illus.; end papers #1.

- Same dedication and contents as 2A.

- The G&D library binding format of 1977 has cover title *The Adventures of Mrs. Peter Rabbit*.

3.   BOWSER THE HOUND — 1920

A.   BURGESS TRADE QUADDIES MARK / Green Meadow Series / [rule] / BOWSER THE HOUND / BY / THORNTON W. BURGESS / With Illustrations by / HARRISON CADY / [pub. logo] / BOSTON / LITTLE, BROWN, AND COMPANY / 1920

- c.1920. Pub. Apr. 1920. Norwood Press. Set up and electrotyped by J. S. Cushing Co., Norwood, Mass.

- [vii]-ix, 1l., [1]-206p., 8 pl. in orange, green, and black incl. front., 20x14cm.

- green cloth on bds.; lettering and design of trees stamped in yellow and dark green; full-col. illus. pasted in center.

- "To the child's loving playmate, loyal protector and staunch ally — the dog, this book is dedicated."

- XLII Chapters. Old Man Coyote leads Bowser the Hound so far from home during a chase that the dog can't find his way back.

B.   BOWSER THE HOUND / BY / THORNTON W. BURGESS / With Illustrations by / HARRISON CADY / GROSSET & DUNLAP / Publishers New York / Printed by arrangement with Little, Brown, and Company

- c.1920 [1st pub. by G&D in 1943].

- [vii]-ix, 1l., [1]-206p., 4 b&w pl. incl. front., 19x12cm.

- blue paper on bds.; lettering stamped in dark blue; d.w. with full-col. illus.; end papers #1.

- Same dedication and contents as 3A.

- The G&D library binding format of 1977 has cover title *The Adventures of Bowser the Hound.*

4.   OLD GRANNY FOX — 1920

A.   BURGESS <u>TRADE</u> QUADDIES <u>MARK</u> / Green Meadow Series / [rule] / OLD GRANNY FOX / BY / THORNTON W. BURGESS / With Illustrations by / HARRISON CADY / [pub. logo] / BOSTON / LITTLE, BROWN, AND COMPANY / 1920

- c.1920. Pub. Sept. 1920.

- [vii]-viii, 1l., [1]-202p., 8 pl. in orange, green, and black incl. front., 20x14cm.

- green cloth on bds.; lettering and design of trees stamped in yellow and dark green; full-col. illus. pasted in center.

- "To the increase of the spirit of mercy and to that gentle charity which before passing judgment on another will seek to get the other's viewpoint, even though that other be but a fox."

- XXIX Chapters. Granny Fox uses her wits to obtain a meal for herself and her grandson Reddy.

B.   OLD GRANNY FOX / BY / THORNTON W. BURGESS / With Illustrations by / HARRISON CADY / GROSSET & DUNLAP / Publishers   New York / Printed by arrangement with Little, Brown, and Company

- c.1920 [1st pub. by G&D in 1943].

- [vii]-viii, 1l., [1]-202p., 4 b&w pl. incl. front., 19x12cm.

- blue paper on bds.; lettering stamped in dark blue, d.w. with full-col. illus.; end papers #1.

- Same dedication and contents as 4A.

- The G&D library binding format of 1977 has cover title *The Adventures of Old Granny Fox.*

1-2-3-4.   THE BURGESS BIG BOOK OF GREEN MEADOW STORIES — 1932

THE BURGESS / BIG / BOOK OF / GREEN MEADOW STORIES / BY / THORNTON W. BURGESS / With Illustrations by / HARRISON CADY / BOSTON / LITTLE, BROWN, AND COMPANY / 1932

- c.1918, 1919, 1920.

- [v]-xii, 1l., 1-204p., 1l., [1]-205p., 1l., [1]-206p., 1l., [1]-202p., pl. in orange, green, and black, incl. front., 21x13cm.

- This book contains the four books in the Green Meadow Series: I. Happy Jack, II. Mrs. Peter Rabbit, III. Bowser the Hound, IV. Old Granny Fox.

Cover of *The Burgess Bird Book for Children*. Boston, Little, Brown c.1919, renewed 1947. Illus. by Louis Agassiz Fuertes.

THE BURGESS NATURAL HISTORY BOOKS FOR CHILDREN (1919-1929)

This Burgess series has no official title, but the four volumes all present natural history in a way that makes it interesting for children to read. The idea to create a bird book for children was suggested to Burgess in 1916, and the author set to work to find a format that would make his book different from the many others that had been written.* His purpose was to interest children in the common species of animal and plant life they could observe for themselves in the wild. Burgess describes the pattern of the four volumes in the statement, "Because there is no method of approach to the child mind equal to the story, this method of conveying information has been adopted."† In each book, a favorite Burgess character sets out to learn facts of nature that before had been unknown to him. As he learns the mysteries of wildlife, so does the child. Burgess enlisted the aid of knowledgeable natural historians in making his books authoritative. The outstanding wildlife artist Louis Agassiz Fuertes painted illustrations for the "Bird" and "Animal" books.

The four books were originally published by Little, Brown and Company. The volumes were brought out in cheaper bindings later. Examples of changes noted are: gold cover lettering and border changed to black, different shades of cloth on bd. covers, and cover paste-on illus. deleted and replaced with a stamp-on design (e.g. "Flower Book"). The "Bird" and "Animal" books came out in Grosset & Dunlap editions in 1965.

The volumes in the series are:

1. The Burgess Bird Book for Children — 1919
2. The Burgess Animal Book for Children — 1920
3. The Burgess Flower Book for Children — 1923
4. The Burgess Seashore Book for Children — 1929

---

*Burgess, *Now I Remember,* p. 117.

†Thornton W. Burgess, "Preface" to *The Burgess Bird Book for Children* (Boston, Little, Brown, 1919), p. xii.

1.   THE BURGESS BIRD BOOK
FOR CHILDREN — 1919

A.   THE BURGESS BIRD BOOK / FOR CHILDREN / BY / THORNTON W. BURGESS / WITH ILLUSTRATIONS IN COLOR BY / LOUIS AGASSIZ FUERTES / [pub. logo] / BOSTON / LITTLE, BROWN, AND COMPANY / 1919

- c.1919. Pub. Oct. 1919. Norwood Press. Set up and electrotyped by J. S. Cushing Co., Norwood, Mass.
- [vi]-xvi, 1l., 351p., 32 full-col. pl. incl. front. (containing 37 pictures, depicting 58 birds), 20x14cm.
- blue cloth on bds.; lettering and illus. border stamped in gold; full-col. illus. of a meadowlark pasted in center; d.w. with same col. illus.
- The book's "primary purpose is to interest the little child in, and to make him acquainted with, those feathered friends he is most likely to see. . . . It is intended to be at once a story book and an authoritative handbook. . . . [The illustrations] were made especially for this volume [by the eminent bird artist L. A. Fuertes]."
- "To the children and the birds of America, that the bonds of love and friendship between them may be strengthened, this book is dedicated."
- XLV Chapters on species of birds of the eastern United States. Peter Rabbit, his curiosity aroused by saucy little Jenny Wren, starts out to investigate the bird world. The familiar Burgess names are given to each bird. Index on pp. 343-351.

B.   *The Burgess Bird Book for Children* was issued by Grosset & Dunlap in 1965 as a companion to its edition of *The Burgess Animal Book for Children* published in the same year. No copy of Grosset's *Bird Book* has been examined, but it is probably in the same format as its *Animal Book,* see p. 73.

2.   THE BURGESS ANIMAL BOOK FOR CHILDREN
— 1920

A.   THE / BURGESS ANIMAL BOOK / FOR CHILDREN / BY / THORNTON W. BURGESS / WITH ILLUSTRATIONS BY / LOUIS AGASSIZ FUERTES / [pub. logo] / BOSTON / LITTLE, BROWN, AND COMPANY / 1920

- c.1920. Pub. Nov. 1920. Norwood Press. Set up and electrotyped by J. S. Cushing Co., Norwood, Mass.
- [vi]-xvii, 363p., 48 pl. incl. front. (containing 73 animal pictures, 154 in col., 19 in b&w), 20x14cm.
- green cloth on bds.; lettering and illus. border stamped in gold and design of trees stamped in dark green; full-col. illus. of a moose pasted in center; d.w. with same col. illus.

- This book is "offered merely as an introduction to the four-footed friends, little and big, which form so important a part of the wildlife of the United States and Canada. . . . The drawings in color and black and white [are] by Mr. Louis Agassiz Fuertes, the artist naturalist. These drawings were made especially for this book."
- "To the Cause of Wild Life in America, especially the mammals many of which are seriously threatened with extinction, this book is dedicated."
- XL Chapters on animal species of North America. When Peter Rabbit learns that his knowledge of animal life is sadly lacking, he and his cousin Jumper the Hare go to school to Old Mother Nature to discover more about their relatives, friends, and neighbors. Index on pp. 355-363.

B.   THE / BURGESS ANIMAL / BOOK / for Children / by / THORNTON W. BURGESS / With Illustrations in Color by / LOUIS AGASSIZ FUERTES / Publishers   GROSSET & DUNLAP   New York

- c.1920,1948 by Thornton W. Burgess. c.1965 by Grosset & Dunlap, Inc. By arrangement with Little, Brown and Company. Published simultaneously in Canada.
- [4]-6-[10]-128p., 8 pages of illus. on glossy paper (containing 61 animal pictures from the original volume; 3,4, or 5 to the page; pictures on both sides of the page; 51 in col., 10 in b&w), 27x20cm.
- tan paper on bds.; gold lettering stamped on cover and spine; d.w. with full-col. illus. of Puma the Panther and lettering in blue, pink, and black.
- Same dedication and preface as 2A. An editor's preface is added. (Since the editor's preface was copyrighted in 1968, it may or may not have appeared in the first printings of this edition.)
- Same contents as 2A, except the index is deleted.

3.   THE BURGESS FLOWER BOOK FOR CHILDREN
— 1923

THE / BURGESS FLOWER BOOK / FOR CHILDREN / BY / THORNTON W. BURGESS / WITH ILLUSTRATIONS / [pub. logo] / BOSTON / LITTLE, BROWN, AND COMPANY / 1923

- c.1923. Pub. May 1923.
- [vi]-xviii, [2]-350p., 48 pl. (32 in color incl. front., 16 in b&w, 103 wildflowers depicted), 20x14cm.
- dark green cloth on bds.; lettering and illus. border stamped in gold, fern design stamped in green; full-col. illus. of mountain laurel pasted in center; d.w. with same col. illus.
- "Its purpose is to awaken and stimulate an interest in our wild flowers. [Credit is given for the photographs] to Mr. L. W. Brownell, Mr. Henry Troth, the J. Horace McFarland Co. and the A. B. Morse Co., and to Miss C. M. Green for her careful work in coloring these photographs."
- "To the awakening in children of love for our wild flowers and the desire to preserve

them in their native habitats for the beauty and joy they give to the world this book is dedicated.''

- XLII Chapters on species of wildflowers. From the skunk cabbage blossom in the early spring to the fringed gentian in the late fall, Peter Rabbit learns about wild flowers of field and forest. Appendix pp. 295-338. Index pp. 339-350.

- A later Little, Brown printing has a binding of light green cloth on bds. with letters stamped in gold and fern design stamped in dark green. (Copy examined was a 1945 printing.)

4.   THE BURGESS SEASHORE BOOK
FOR CHILDREN — 1929

THE / BURGESS SEASHORE BOOK / FOR CHILDREN / BY / THORNTON W. BURGESS / WITH ILLUSTRATIONS BY / W. H. SOUTHWICK AND GEORGE SUTTON / [pub. logo] / BOSTON / LITTLE, BROWN, AND COMPANY / 1929

- c.1929. Pub. Oct. 1929.

- [vi]-xiv, [2]-336p., 48 pl. (32 in col. incl. front.), 20x14cm.

- blue cloth on bds., lettering and illus. border stamped in gold and design of seaweed stamped in green, paper illus. of three-spined stickleback pasted in center, d.w. with same col. illus.

- ''[This book is] an introduction to the life of the seashore. . . . It is intended to be at once a storybook and a handbook. . . . those things most frequently seen along the Atlantic coast have been selected. . . . American Museum of Natural History [furnished] photographs, W. H. Southwick [drew the sea life], George N. Sutton the drawings of seashore birds.''

- ''To Robert, Frances, Rosemary, and Jean.''

- XL Chapters on forms of life around the seashore. Danny Meadow Mouse is accidentally carried by aeroplane to the seashore and learns about the life there. Appendix pp. 295-330. Index pp. 331-336.

GREEN FOREST SERIES (1921-1923)

More Burgess characters become the subjects of their own books. The format is the same as that of the Green Meadow Series, only this time the subjects all live in the Green Forest. The stories first appeared in Burgess's newspaper story column.

The editions of the Green Forest Series have undergone the same changes in reprintings as the Green Meadow Series. The Grosset & Dunlap new binding version of about 1962 was done on orange paper. Again the cover titles of the library bindings of 1977 had the words "The Adventures of . . ." added.

The books in the series are:

1. Lightfoot the Deer — 1921
2. Blacky the Crow — 1922
3. Whitefoot the Wood Mouse — 1922
4. Buster Bear's Twins — 1923

1. LIGHTFOOT THE DEER — 1921

A. BURGESS TRADE QUADDIES MARK / Green Forest Series / [rule] / LIGHTFOOT THE DEER / BY / THORNTON W. BURGESS / With Illustrations by / HARRISON CADY / [pub. logo] / BOSTON / LITTLE, BROWN, AND COMPANY / 1921

- c.1921. Pub. Apr. 1921. Set up and electrotyped by J. S. Cushing Co., Norwood, Mass.

- [vii]-viii, 1l., [1]-205p., 8 pl. in orange, green, and black incl. front., 20x14cm.

- blue cloth on bds.; paper pasted on cover contains black lettering, background picture of a forest, and a color illus. in the center.

- "To the most beautiful of our four-footed friends in the Green Forest with the hope that this little volume may in some degree aid in the protection of the innocent and helpless."

- XL Chapters. This anti-hunting book shows the terrors of deer hunting from the deer's point of view.

B.   LIGHTFOOT THE DEER / BY / THORNTON W. BURGESS / With Illustrations by / HARRISON CADY / GROSSET & DUNLAP / Publishers New York / Printed by arrangement with Little, Brown, and Company

- c.1921 [1st pub. by G&D in 1944].

- [vii]-viii, 1l., [1]-205p., 4 b&w pl. incl. front., 19x12cm.

- blue paper on bds.; lettering stamped in dark blue; d.w. with full-col. illus.; end papers #1.

- Same dedication and contents as 1A.

- The G&D library binding format of 1977 has cover title *The Adventures of Lightfoot the Deer*. In conjunction with this printing, the book was issued in paperback, tempo books, Grosset & Dunlap, [vii]-viii, 2l., [1]-205p., 4 pl. in line drawings, yellow paper covers with col. illus.

2.   BLACKY THE CROW — 1922

A.   BURGESS TRADE QUADDIES MARK / Green Forest Series / [rule] / BLACKY THE CROW / BY / THORNTON W. BURGESS / With Illustrations by / HARRISON CADY / [pub. logo] / BOSTON / LITTLE, BROWN, AND COMPANY / 1922

- c.1922. Pub. Apr. 1922.

- [vii]-viii, 1l., [1]-206p., 8 pl. in orange, green, and black, incl. front., 20x14cm.

- blue cloth on bds.; paper pasted on cover contains black lettering, background picture of a forest, and a col. illus. in center.

- "To an American citizen, who despite persecution and changed conditions, has by his adaptibility and intelligence maintained his place in the land of his forefathers — the crow."

- XXXII Chapters. Rascally Blacky the Crow uses his smartness to torment Hooty the Owl, save some ducks from hunters, and to try to crack a china egg.

B.   BLACKY THE CROW / BY / THORNTON W. BURGESS / With Illustrations by / HARRISON CADY / GROSSET & DUNLAP / Publishers   New York / Printed by arrangement with Little, Brown, and Company

- c.1922 [1st pub. by G&D in 1944].

- [vii]-viii, 1l., [1]-206p., 4 b&w pl. incl. front., 19x12cm.

Cover of *Lightfoot the Deer* (Green Forest Series). Boston, Little, Brown, c. 1921. Illus by Harrison Cady.

- blue paper on bds.; lettering stamped in dark blue; d.w. with full-col. illus.; end papers #1.
- Same dedication and contents as 2A.
- The G&D library binding format of 1977 has cover title *The Adventures of Blacky the Crow.*

3.   WHITEFOOT THE WOOD MOUSE — 1922

A.   BURGESS <u>TRADE</u> QUADDIES <u>MARK</u> / Green Forest Series / [rule] / WHITEFOOT / THE WOOD MOUSE / BY / THORNTON W. BURGESS / With Illustrations by / HARRISON CADY / [pub. logo] / BOSTON / LITTLE, BROWN, AND COMPANY / 1922

- c.1922. Pub. Oct. 1922.
- [v]-vi, 1l., [1]-181p., 8 pl. done in orange, green, and black, 20x14cm.
- blue cloth on bds.; paper pasted on cover contains black lettering, background picture of a forest, and a col. illus. in the center.
- XXXII Chapters. Whitefoot spends one winter in Farmer Brown's sugar house and another in the Green Forest escaping such enemies as Whitey the Snowy Owl, Shadow the Weasel, and Butcher the Shrike. Little Miss Dainty becomes Mrs. Whitefoot.

B.   WHITEFOOT / THE WOOD MOUSE / BY / THORNTON W. BURGESS / With Illustrations by / HARRISON CADY / GROSSET & DUNLAP / Publishers New York / Printed by arrangement with Little, Brown, and Company

- c.1922 [1st pub. by G&D in 1944].
- [v]-vi, 1l., [1]-181p., 4 b&w pl. incl. front., 19x12cm.
- blue paper on bds.; lettering stamped in dark blue; d.w. with col. illus.; end papers #1.
- Same contents as 3A.
- The orange binding version of about 1962 contains only 180p. The library binding format of 1977 has cover title *The Adventures of Whitefoot the Wood Mouse.*

4.   BUSTER BEAR'S TWINS — 1923

A.   BURGESS <u>TRADE</u> QUADDIES <u>MARK</u> /Green Forest Series / [rule] / BUSTER BEAR'S TWINS / BY / THORNTON W. BURGESS / With Illustrations by / HARRISON CADY / [pub. logo] / BOSTON / LITTLE, BROWN, AND COMPANY / 1923

- c.1921,1923. Pub. Oct. 1923.

- [vii]-viii, 1l., [1]-207p., 8 pl. in orange, green, and black incl. front., 20x14cm.

- blue cloth on bds.; paper pasted on cover contains black lettering, a background picture of a forest, and a col. illus. in center.

- "To childhood, little human folk, little people in fur and feathers and all other children of Old Mother Nature this book is dedicated."

- XXXIV Chapters. Boxer and Woof-Woof, Buster Bear's twin cubs, must learn many lessons from Mother Bear before they can make their own way in the Great World.

B. BUSTER BEAR'S TWINS / BY / THORNTON W. BURGESS / With Illustrations by / HARRISON CADY / GROSSET & DUNLAP / Publishers New York / Printed by arrangement with Little, Brown, and Company

- c.1921, 1923. [1st pub. by G&D in 1944].

- [vii]-viii, 1l., [1]-207p., 8 pl. in orange, green, and black incl. front., 20x14cm.

- blue cloth on bds.; lettering stamped in dark blue; d.w. with col. illus.; end papers #1.

- Same dedication and contents as 4A.

- The library binding of 1977 has cover title *The Adventures of Buster Bear's Twins*.

Cover of *Billy Mink* (Smiling Pool Series). Boston, Little, Brown, c.1924, renewed 1952 by Thornton W. Burgess. Illus. by Harrison Cady.

SMILING POOL SERIES (1924-1927)

This group of four books published by Little, Brown and Company rounds out the books on individual animals. The stories, about the inhabitants of the Smiling Pool, first appeared in Burgess's newspaper story column.

The Grosset & Dunlap editions, which came out in 1946, went through several printing changes from the first printing (described in this bibliography). The changes include several forms of the Grosset end papers, covers of a different texture and shade of green, and the plates on glossy paper redrawn in line drawings and printed on the regular text paper. The new binding editions of about 1962 were done in purple paper on boards with no d.w. (the original d.w. illus. printed on the cover). The words "The Adventures of . . ." preceded the four titles on the covers of the 1977 library binding editions.

The four books in the series are:
1. Billy Mink - 1924
2. Little Joe Otter - 1925
3. Jerry Muskrat at Home - 1926
4. Longlegs the Heron - 1927

1.   BILLY MINK — 1924

A.   BURGESS TRADE QUADDIES MARK / Smiling Pool Series / [rule] / BILLY MINK / BY / THORNTON W. BURGESS / With Illustrations by / HARRISON CADY / [pub. logo] / BOSTON / LITTLE, BROWN, AND COMPANY / 1924

- c.1919, 1920, 1924. Pub. Sept. 1924.
- [v]-vi, 1l., [1]-196p., 8 pl. in orange, green, and black incl. front., 20x14cm.
- olive green cloth on bds.; paper pasted on cover contains lettering in orange, background illus. of a pond, and col. illus. in the center.
- XL Chapters. Billy Mink leaves the Smiling Pool and goes to hunt rats in a farmer's barn.

B. BURGESS TRADE QUADDIES MARK / Smiling Pool Series / [rule] / Billy Mink / By / THORNTON W. BURGESS / With Illustrations by / HARRISON CADY / [pub. logo] / [rule] / Grosset & Dunlap / PUBLISHERS NEW YORK

- c.1919, 1920, 1924. By arrangement with Little, Brown, and Company [1st pub. by G&D in 1946].
- [v]-vi, 1l.,[1]-196p., 4 b&w pl. incl. front., 19x12cm.
- green paper on bds.; illus. on cover and lettering on spine stamped in black; d.w. with col. illus.; end papers #1.
- Same contents as 1A.
- The library binding of 1977 has cover title *The Adventures of Billy Mink.*

2.   LITTLE JOE OTTER — 1925

A.   BURGESS TRADE QUADDIES MARK / Smiling Pool Series / [rule] / LITTLE JOE OTTER / BY / THORNTON W. BURGESS / With Illustrations by / HARRISON CADY / [pub. logo] / BOSTON / LITTLE, BROWN, AND COMPANY / 1925

- c.1925.
- [v]-vi, 1l., [1]-198p., 8 pl. in orange, green and black incl. front., 20x14cm.
- olive green cloth on bds.; paper pasted on cover contains lettering in orange, background illus. of a pond, and color illus. in center.
- XXXIV Chapters. Little Joe Otter's two youngsters learn the ways of life.

B.   BURGESS TRADE QUADDIES MARK / Smiling Pool Series / [rule] / Little Joe Otter / By / THORNTON W. BURGESS / With Illustrations by / HARRISON CADY / [pub. logo] / [rule] / Grosset & Dunlap / PUBLISHERS NEW YORK

- c.1925. By arrangement with Little, Brown and Company [1st pub. by G&D in 1946].
- [v]-vi, 1l., [1]-198p., 4 b&w pl. incl. front., 19x12cm.
- green paper on bds.; illus on cover and lettering on spine stamped in black; d.w. with col.illus.; end papers #1.
- Same contents as 2A.
- The G&D library binding format of 1977 has cover title *The Adventures of Little Joe Otter.* In conjunction with this printing, the book was issued in paperback edition under the title *The Adventures of Little Joe Otter,* tempo books, Grosset & Dunlap, 2 p.l., [1]-198p., illus. in line drawings, yellow paper covers with col. cover illus.

3.   JERRY MUSKRAT AT HOME — 1926

A.   BURGESS <u>TRADE</u> QUADDIES <u>MARK</u> / Smiling Pool Series / [rule] / JERRY MUSKRAT AT HOME / BY / THORNTON W. BURGESS / With Illustrations by / HARRISON CADY / [pub. logo] / BOSTON / LITTLE, BROWN, AND COMPANY / 1926

- c.1918, 1926.
- [v]-vi, 1l., [1]-206p., 8 pl. in orange, green, and black incl. front., 20x14cm.
- olive green cloth on bds.; paper pasted on cover contains lettering in orange, background illus. of a pond, and color illus. in center.
- XXXVIII Chapters. First Reddy Fox and then a trapper try to lure Jerry from his home so they can catch him.

B.   BURGESS <u>TRADE</u> QUADDIES <u>MARK</u> / Smiling Pool Series / [rule] / Jerry Muskrat / at Home / By / THORNTON W. BURGESS / With Illustrations by / HARRISON CADY / [pub. logo] / [rule] / Grosset & Dunlap / PUBLISHERS   NEW YORK

- c.1918, 1926. By arrangement with Little, Brown and Company [1st pub. by G&D in 1946].
- [v]-vi, 1l., [1]-206p., 4 b&w pl. incl., front., 19x12cm.
- green paper on bds.; illus. on cover and lettering on spine stamped in black; d.w. with full-col. illus., end papers #1.
- Same contents as 3A.
- The G&D library binding format of 1977 has cover title *The Adventures of Jerry Muskrat at Home.*

4.   LONGLEGS THE HERON — 1927

A.   BURGESS <u>TRADE</u> QUADDIES <u>MARK</u> / Smiling Pool Series / [rule] / LONGLEGS / THE HERON / BY / THORNTON W. BURGESS / With Illustrations by / HARRISON CADY / [pub. logo] / BOSTON / LITTLE, BROWN, AND COMPANY / 1927

- c.1916, 1921, 1927. Pub. Sept. 1927.
- [v]-vi, 1l., [1]-207p., 8 pl. in orange, green, and black incl. front., 20x14cm.
- olive green cloth on bds.; paper illus. on cover contains orange lettering, background picture of a pond, and color illus. in center.
- XXXIII Chapters. Peter Rabbit saves Grandfather Frog from Longlegs, and a young heron catches his foot in a trap.

B.   BURGESS ^{TRADE} QUADDIES ^{MARK} / Smiling Pool Series / [rule] / Longlegs / The Heron / By / THORNTON W. BURGESS / With Illustrations by / HARRISON CADY / [pub. logo] / [rule] / Grosset & Dunlap / PUBLISHERS   NEW YORK

- c.1916, 1921, 1927. By arrangement with Little, Brown, and Company [1st pub. by G&D in 1946].

- [v]-vi, 1l., [1]-207p., 4 b&w pl. incl. front., 19x12cm.

- green paper on bds.; illus. on cover and lettering on spine stamped in black; d.w. with col. illus.; end papers #1.

- Same contents as 4A.

- The G&D library binding format of 1977 has cover title *The Adventures of Longlegs the Heron.*

Cover of *The Christmas Reindeer*. New York, The MacMillan Co., c.1926.

THE CHRISTMAS REINDEER (1926)

THE CHRISTMAS / REINDEER / BY / THORNTON W. BURGESS / IL-
LUSTRATED BY / RHODA CHASE / New York / THE MACMILLAN COM-
PANY / 1926 / All rights reserved

- c.1926. Pub. Oct., 1926.

- 5 p.l., [2]-139p., 7 b&w pl. incl. front., several b&w line illus., 17x11cm.

- red cloth on bds.; lettering stamped in gold; illus. of Santa Claus and reindeer on
  end papers; d.w. in gray, pink, and black, with black lettering.

- "To the beautiful faith of childhood."

- XXIII Chapters. A make-believe adventure mixed with true facts about reindeer.
  An Eskimo girl is taken by her pet reindeer, Whitefoot, to Kringle Valley. One of
  the few books which does not contain the familiar Burgess characters and settings.

- Also issued by Book League of America, 1929.

BIRDS YOU SHOULD KNOW (1933)

Birds / You Should Know / By / THORNTON W. BURGESS / Author of
"The Burgess Bird Book for Children" / And Other Nature Books / Colored
Illustrations / By / LOUIS AGASSIZ FUERTES / Reproduced by Permission of
the Board of Regents / of the State of New York, from Original / Paintings in
Possession of the / State Museum / BOSTON / LITTLE, BROWN, AND
COMPANY / 1933

Cover of *Birds You Should Know*. Boston, Little, Brown, c.1933.

- c.1933. Printed by J. B. Lyon Co., Albany, N.Y.

- [3]-256p., 144 bird illustrations (many full-page, many 2 illus. on a page), 14x10cm.

- black simulated leather, title and illus. stamped in gold.

- "This book is offered as an introduction to and aid in identification of common land birds and some of the rarer species, together with a few shore and water birds, likely to be encountered east of the Mississippi River. . . ."

- This book is strictly a natural history; no plot; no Burgess characters. The colored illus. of the birds appears on the verso of each page and the brief description on the facing recto.

- The New York State Education Department commissioned Louis Agassiz Fuertes to illustrate the two volume work *Birds of New York* by Elon Howard Eaton (Albany, University of New York, 1910, 1914). Selections from these paintings and portions of paintings appear as the illustrations of *Birds You Should Know*.

THE BOOK OF ANIMAL LIFE (1937)

THE / BOOK OF ANIMAL LIFE / By / THORA STOWELL / and / THORNTON W. BURGESS / [illus. of an elephant] / WITH ILLUSTRATIONS / BOSTON / LITTLE, BROWN AND COMPANY / 1937

- First edition pub. Mar. 1937.

- 6 p.l., [3]-315p., 16 pl. containing 38 photographs and many other b&w drawings, 20x14cm.

- green cloth on bds., lettering and illus. stamped in brown, green d.w. with black lettering and illus. of a bear.

- "[This book] has been written in a spirit of reverence for the Creator of all life in whose all-wise plan the animals, as we commonly call mammals other than man, have a hardly less important place than man."

- "To Michael Stowell and his friends at Normandale Preparatory School."

- XX Chapters on various topics concerning animals of the world. The book is strictly an informational book with no Burgess plot or characters.

- Thora Stowell is the pseudonym of Alice Mary Dicken. Mrs. Dicken's original volume, *The Book of Animal Life*, was published in 1935 by G. G. Harrap & Co. of London. Burgess wrote additional material for the book's American edition published by Little, Brown & Co.

Dust wrapper of *While the Story-Log Burns*. Boston, Little, Brown, c.1938, renewed 1966 by Louis Doherty and the Third National Bank, Hampden County, Mass., executors of the estate of Thornton W. Burgess. Illus. by Lemuel Palmer.

TALES FROM THE STORYTELLER'S HOUSE
and WHILE THE STORY-LOG BURNS (1937-1938)

These two books, while not properly called a series, form a pair. They both have the same format and were illustrated in the Little, Brown editions by Lemuel Palmer. The setting of both books is the Old House near Esker Hill where the Old Storyteller lived. In the evening a story-log was placed in the Storyteller's fireplace and a group of eager children would gather around.

> You don't know what a story-log is? Why, it is a log that burns while a story is being told. . . . On each story night there at the Old House a boy or girl brought a small log. With proper ceremony this was placed on the fire. While it burned the Storyteller must tell a story.*

The stories in this collection are all taken from other sources, and the framework of the Storyteller and children is added. The Storyteller's house is Burgess's house in Hampden, Mass. The Storyteller (who is like Burgess himself) tells most of the stories; others are by the children, while an Old Hunter relates true incidents, and a Naturalist dispenses nature facts. Most of the stories are about the traditional Burgess characters; some (from the *People's Home Journal*) are the familiar Burgess legends.

Grosset & Dunlap brought out the books in one volume called *The Big Thornton Burgess Storybook*. It contained no illustrations other than the full color one on the dust wrapper.

1.   Tales from the Storyteller's House - 1937
2.   While the Story-Log Burns - 1938
1-2.   The Big Thornton Burgess Storybook - 1950

---

*Thornton W. Burgess, *Tales from the Storyteller's House* (Boston, Little, Brown, 1937), p.9.

1. TALES FROM THE STORYTELLER'S HOUSE
— 1937

TALES FROM / THE STORYTELLER'S HOUSE / BY THORNTON W. BURGESS / [pub. logo] / With Illustrations by / LEMUEL PALMER / BOSTON / LITTLE, BROWN AND COMPANY / 1937

- c.1937. Pub. Nov. 1937.

- 6 p.l., [2]-195p., 8 full-page col. illus. incl. front., 21x16cm.

- tan cloth on bds., lettering stamped in orange, white d.w. with col. illus.

- "There are certain facts in connection with the stories in this volume that may be of interest to the reader. The Old House which furnishes the setting was built in 1742. For several years it has been my summer home. The hill immediately behind it is a splendid example of that peculiar formation made by deposits of gravel or sand by a subglacial stream and known as an Esker. Laughing Brook flows along its base on the east. Several of the stories appeared years ago in *Red Cross Magazine*, which, having served its purpose, ceased publication shortly after the World War. Other stories were published in the *People's Home Journal*. The stories told by the Old Hunter are true stories, actual incidents which occurred just as described and were furnished me by eyewitnesses. 'The Joy of the Beautiful Pine' was written for the exercises with which my home city celebrated Christmas with its first municipal Christmas tree."

- "To All My Grandchildren and to all other children who love stories these tales from Old Mother Nature are dedicated."

- I. The Old House [gives the setting and framework of the book]
  II. The Most Precious Thing in the World [first appeared in *People's Home Journal*, Sept. 1926, p.37, under the title "Peter Rabbit Finds the Thing Without Price"]
  III. Why the Green Forest Has No King [*PHJ*, Feb. 1926, p. 4, under title "Why There is No King in the Green Forest"]
  IV. Cold Toes and a New Tail [*PHJ*, May 1920, p. 54, under title "Old Mr. Fox's New Tail"]
  V. The Old Hunter's Story [the 1st story told by the Old Hunter]
  VI. The Opened Eyes [first appeared in *Red Cross Magazine*, XV (July 1920), 30-32, under title "Old Mr. Toad Opens Peter Rabbit's Eyes"]
  VII. Mrs. Possum's Big Pocket [*PHJ*, June 1921, p. 38, under title "How Mrs. Possum Got Her Pocket"]
  VIII. Truth about Reddy [an Old Hunter true story]
  IX. The Long Look Ahead [*PHJ*, Mar. 1926, p. 3, under the title "Paddy's Long Look Ahead"]
  X. Fussy Folk
  XI. The Story of Big Feet [*PHJ*, Aug. 1924, p. 31, under the title "Why Tufty the Lynx Has Big Feet"]
  XII. The Handiest Tongue [*PHJ*, Aug. 1921, p. 34, under title "Why Old Mr. Toad's Tongue is Hind-Side Before"]
  XIII. It Really Happened [an Old Hunter true story]

XIV.	The Fox and the Seal [*PHJ*, Nov. 1926, p. 40, under title "Reddy Fox Meets Barker the Seal"]
 XV.	A Wonderful and Beautiful Discovery [*Red Cross Magazine*, XV (June 1920), 13-15, under title "Peter Rabbit Discovers a Wonderful Thing"]
XVI.	The Joy of the Beautiful Pine [see foreword above]

# 2.	WHILE THE STORY-LOG BURNS — 1938

WHILE / THE STORY-LOG / BURNS / BY THORNTON W. BURGESS / [pub. logo] / With Illustrations by / LEMUEL PALMER / BOSTON / LITTLE, BROWN AND COMPANY / 1938

- c.1938. Pub. Oct. 1938.

- 6 p.l., [2]-194-[195]p., 8 full-page col. illus. incl. front., 21x16cm.

- green cloth on bds., lettering stamped in red, white d.w. with col. illus.

- "To nature lovers of all ages this book is dedicated."

- I.	The Children's Hour
  II.	The Rarest Thing in the World [first appeared in *People's Home Journal*, Oct. 1923, p.54 +]
  III.	The Old Naturalist [a Naturalist talks to the children]
  IV.	The Whistler [*PHJ*, Jul. - Aug. 1920, p.42, under title "The Marmot Family Whistle"]
  V.	Frances Tells a Story [*PHJ*, June 1923, p.46 + , under title "How Old Mr. Crow Used His Wits"]
  VI.	Grandpa Pelican's Fish Bag [*PHJ*, Dec. 1918, p.38 + , under title "How Grandpa Pelican Came By His Big Fish Bag"]
  VII.	The Question-Log [nature facts from the Naturalist]
  VIII.	Thunderer Saves a Friend [*PHJ*, Mar. 1923, p.58 + , under title "Mrs. Grouse Saves Jumper the Hare"]
  IX.	Peter and Paddy [*Red Cross Magazine*, XV (Oct. 1920), p.27-30, under title "Peter Gets a New Idea"]
  X.	Tribute to the King [*PHJ*, Jul. 1922, p.38 + , under title "How Plunger Had to Pay Tribute"]
  XI.	The Shrews and the Whale [nature facts from the Naturalist]
  XII.	An Independent Gentleman [*PHJ*, Oct. 1926, p.40, under title "Where Jimmy Skunk got his Independence"]
  XIII.	The Closing of a Door [*PHJ*, Mar. 1920, p.58, under title "Striped Chipmunk's Sly Trick"]
  XIV.	The Story of a Beautiful Coat [*PHJ*, Oct. 1921, p.50 + , under title "How Mother Nature Took Pity on Flamecoat"]
  XV.	Everybody's Night [contains true stories including the Old Hunter's]
  XVI.	Buster Bear's Sugar Party

1-2. THE BIG THORNTON BURGESS STORY-BOOK — 1950

THE BIG / THORNTON BURGESS / STORY-BOOK / TALES FROM THE STORYTELLER'S HOUSE / WHILE THE STORY-LOG BURNS / By / Thornton W. Burgess / [design] / Grosset & Dunlap / PUBLISHERS • NEW YORK

- c.1937, 1938. Under titles *Tales from the Storyteller's House* and *While the Story-Log Burns*. By arrangement with Little, Brown & Co. [pub. by G&D in 1950].

- 5 p.l., [2]-195, [2]-194-[195]p., no illus., 23x15cm.

- blue cloth on bds., lettering on spine stamped in black, blue d.w. with col. illus. of the Storyteller surrounded by children and animals (no illustrator given).

- Dedication and foreword are from *Tales from the Story-Teller's House*.

- I. Tales from the Story-Teller's House,   II. While the Story-Log Burns.

BOOKS OF NATURE STORIES (1944-1950)

The six books in this series all have the subtitle "A Book of Nature Stories." Each book concentrates on the happenings in one of the settings in the Burgess world, such as the Smiling Pool or the Green Meadows. Unusual and little known facts about wildlife are brought out through the stories.

Five books of the series came out in three collected editions of two books in a volume. Little, Brown published *Along Laughing Brook. On the Green Meadows,* and Grosset and Dunlap published *The Big Book of Burgess Nature Stories* and *50 Favorite Burgess Stories.* (The book *At Paddy the Beaver's Pond* did not come out in a collected edition, but *On the Green Meadows* came out in two.) The Grosset books used the original series design, a silhouette of Peter Rabbit encircled by his friends, on the cover, but did not use the original end papers or color illustrations.

Bonanza Books brought out at least one of the six books (*At Paddy the Beaver's Pond*) in a reduced-size reprint.

The books of the series are:

1. On the Green Meadows — 1944
2. At the Smiling Pool — 1945
3. The Crooked Little Path — 1946
4. The Dear Old Briar Patch — 1947
5. Along Laughing Brook — 1949
6. At Paddy the Beaver's Pond — 1950

5-1. Along Laughing Brook. On the Green Meadows — 1954
2-4. The Big Book of Burgess Nature Stories — 1955
1-3. 50 Favorite Burgess Stories — 1956

1.   ON THE GREEN MEADOWS — 1944

ON THE / GREEN MEADOWS / A Book of Nature Stories by / THORNTON

W. BURGESS / Illustrated by / HARRISON CADY / LITTLE, BROWN AND COMPANY / BOSTON • 1944 / [illus. (covering the preceding page and part of the title page)]

- c.1944. Pub. Oct. 1944.
- 4 p.l., [2]-182p., 4 pl. done in b&w & green, many b&w illus., 21x16cm.
- green cloth on bds.; lettering and series design stamped in black; d.w. with illus. in 3 col.; illus. end papers done in green.
- XXVIII Chapters. Stories about the animals who live on the Green Meadows.

2.   AT THE SMILING POOL — 1945

AT / THE / SMILING POOL / A Book of Nature Stories by / THORNTON W. BURGESS / Illustrated by / HARRISON CADY / LITTLE, BROWN AND COMPANY / BOSTON • 1945 / [illus. (covering the preceding page and part of the title page)]

- c.1945. Pub. May 1945.
- 4 p.l., [2]-184-[185]p., 4 pl. in b&w & blue, 8 b&w pl., many b&w illus. incl. several full-page, 21x16cm.
- red cloth on bds.; lettering and series design stamped in black; d.w. with illus. in 3 col.; illus. end papers done in blue.
- XXVIII Chapters. Stories about muskrats, frogs, kingfishers and other denizens of the Smiling Pool.

3.   THE CROOKED LITTLE PATH — 1946

THE CROOKED / LITTLE PATH / A Book of Nature Stories by / THORN-TON W. BURGESS / Illustrated by / HARRISON CADY / LITTLE, BROWN AND COMPANY / BOSTON • 1946 / [illus. (covering the preceding page and part of the title page)]

- c.1946. Pub. Apr. 1946.
- 4 p.l., [2]-184p., 4 pl. done in b&w & yellow, 7 b&w pl., many other b&w illus., 21x16cm. (Bonanza books reprint, 18x14cm.)
- red cloth on bds.; lettering stamped in black; d.w. with illus. in 3 col.; illus. end papers done in yellow.
- XXVI Chapters. Stories about the woodland folk who travel along the Crooked Little Path.

4.   THE DEAR OLD BRIAR-PATCH — 1947

THE DEAR OLD / BRIAR-PATCH / A Book of Nature Stories by / THORN-

Cover of *The Crooked Little Path*. Boston, Little, Brown, c.1946, renewed 1974 by Louis Doherty and the Third National Bank, Hampden County, Mass., executors of the estate of Thornton W. Burgess.

TON W. BURGESS / Illustrated by / HARRISON CADY / LITTLE, BROWN AND COMPANY / BOSTON • 1947 / [illus. (covering the preceding page and part of the title page)]

- c.1947. Pub. Aug. 1947. Published simultaneously in Canada by McClelland and Stewart Limited.
- 5 p.l., [2]-185p., 4 pl. done in b&w & red, 6 b&w pl., many b&w illus., 21x16cm.
- red cloth on bds.; lettering and series design stamped in black; d.w. with illus. in 2 col.; illus. end papers done in red.
- XXV Chapters. Peter Rabbit finds that the Dear Old Briar-Patch provides homes for many others besides himself and his family.

5.   ALONG LAUGHING BROOK — 1949

ALONG / LAUGHING BROOK / A Book of Nature Stories by / THORN-TON W. BURGESS / Illustrated by / HARRISON CADY / LITTLE, BROWN AND COMPANY / BOSTON • 1949 / [illus. (covering preceding page and part of the title page)]

- c.1949. Pub. Mar. 1949. Published simultaneously in Canada by McClelland and Stewart Limited.
- 4 p.l., [2]-150p., 7 full-page b&w illus., many other b&w illus., 21x16cm.
- red cloth on bds.; lettering and series design stamped in black; d.w. with illus. in 2 col.; illus. end papers done in blue.
- XXI Chapters. Stories of animals who live along the Laughing Brook.

6.   AT PADDY THE BEAVER'S POND — 1950

AT PADDY THE / BEAVER'S POND / A Book of Nature Stories by / THORNTON W. BURGESS / Illustrated by / HARRISON CADY / LITTLE, BROWN AND COMPANY / BOSTON • 1950 / [illus. (covering the preceding page and part of the title page)]

- c.1950. Pub. May 1950. Published simultaneously in Canada by McClelland and Stewart Limited.
- 5 p.l., [2]-146p., 1l., 7 full-page b&w illus., many other b&w illus., 21x16cm.
- orange cloth on bds.; lettering and series design stamped in black; d.w. with illus. done in orange and black; illus. end papers done in orange.
- XXI Chapters. Stories about life around the beaver pond deep in the Green Forest, at the foot of Great Mountain. The animal species found there are basically northern species such as beaver, moose, Canada goose, Canada jay, and raven.
- A facsimile of *At Paddy the Beaver's Pond* was published by Bonanza Books, New York, a division of Crown Publishers, 18x14cm.

5-1.   ALONG LAUGHING BROOK.
ON THE GREEN MEADOWS — 1954

Along Laughing Brook / • / On the Green Meadows / by THORNTON W. BURGESS / Illustrated by / HARRISON CADY / LITTLE, BROWN AND COMPANY / BOSTON / [illus.]

- c.1944, 1949 [Pub. by Little, Brown in 1954].
- 5 p.l., [2]-150, 5 l., [2]-182p., many b&w and b&w & blue illus., 21x16cm.
- gray cloth on bds.; blue lettering stamped on spine; d.w. with illus. in black, white, and blue; illus. end papers done in blue.
- I. Along Laughing Brook, II. On the Green Meadows.

2-4.   THE BIG BOOK OF BURGESS
NATURE STORIES — 1955

THE BIG BOOK OF / Burgess Nature Stories / AT THE SMILING POOL and / THE DEAR OLD BRIAR-PATCH / BY / THORNTON W. BURGESS / Illustrated by / HARRISON CADY / PUBLISHERS / Grosset & Dunlap / NEW YORK

- *At the Smiling Pool* c.1945, *The Dear Old Briar Patch* c. 1947. By arrangement with Little, Brown & Co. [1st pub. by G&D in 1955].
- 3 p.l., [2]-184-[185], 1l., [2]-185p., many b&w illus. incl. some full-page, 21x16cm.
- gray cloth on bds. and green cloth on bds. varieties; lettering on spine stamped in gold, series design on cover; yellow d.w. with col. illus.
- I. At the Smiling Pool,   II. The Dear Old Briar Patch.

1-3.   50 FAVORITE BURGESS STORIES — 1956

50 FAVORITE / Burgess Stories / ON THE GREEN MEADOWS and / THE CROOKED LITTLE PATH / By / THORNTON W. BURGESS / Illustrated by / HARRISON CADY / PUBLISHERS / Grosset & Dunlap / NEW YORK

- *On the Green Meadows* c.1944, *The Crooked Little Path* c.1946. By arrangement with Little, Brown and Co. [1st pub. by G&D in 1956].
- 3 p.l., [2]-182, 1 l., [2]-184p., many b&w illus. incl. some full-page, 21x16cm.
- gray cloth on bds. and green cloth on bds. varieties; lettering on spine stamped in gold, series design on cover; green d.w. with col. illus.
- I. On the Green Meadows,   II. The Crooked Little Path.

Dust wrapper of *Aunt Sally's Friends in Fur*. Boston, Little, Brown, c. 1955 by Thornton W. Burgess.

AUNT SALLY'S FRIENDS IN FUR (1955)

Aunt Sally's / Friends in Fur / or The Woodhouse Night Club / by THORN-TON W. BURGESS / With 34 Photographs by the Author / LITTLE, BROWN AND COMPANY / Boston • Toronto

- c.1955. Published simultaneously in Canada.
- 4 p.l., [2]-146p., 34 photo. incl. front., 19x13cm.
- green cloth on bds., lettering stamped in yellow, yellow d.w. with brown and blue lettering and brown photo. of animals.
- "To Alice Rebecca Cooke, Understanding friend and protector of lesser folk in fur and feathers."
- 14 Chapters. A true story about an old lady and the experiences she has feeding wild animals, mostly skunks and raccoons, that come to visit her woodshed.
- Aunt Sally's real name was Alice Rebecca Cooke of Sandwich, Mass. (born 1861, died 1956).* "During the thirties, Thornton W. Burgess obtained lots of [movie] footage [of Miss Cooke and the animals] and the movies of these scenes became an important part of the appealing lecture package he had put together."† "The woodshed night club was discontinued in 1947, due to extensive hunting of the animals near Alice's house, and to her failing health."°

---

*Lovell, pp. 75 & 82.
†*Ibid.*, p. 79.
°*Ibid.*, p. 82.

Cover of *Read Aloud Peter Rabbit Stories*. New York, Wonder Books, c.1958. Cover illus. by Pauline Jackson from *How Peter Cottontail Got His Name*. New York, Wonder Books, c.1957.

WONDER READ ALOUD BOOKS (1958-1965)

Wonder Books, a division of Grosset & Dunlap, created a series of Read Aloud Books, of which three were by Thornton W. Burgess. The stories, selected by Dr. Margaret Bittner Parke, Dr. May Lazar, and Margaret C. Farquhar, are meant for parents to read aloud to their children. The Burgess books in the series are:

1. Read Aloud Peter Rabbit Stories - 1958
2. Nature Stories to Read Aloud - 1959
3. Mother West Wind Stories to Read Aloud - 1965

1. READ ALOUD PETER RABBIT STORIES — 1958

READ [Wonder Books symbol] ALOUD / PETER RABBIT / STORIES / By THORNTON W. BURGESS / Illustrated by ELIZABETH MONATH / [illus.] / WONDER BOOKS • NEW YORK

- c.1958.
- [4]-160p., many b&w illus., 20x13cm.
- yellow paper covers; black, red and yellow lettering; full-col. illus. [by Pauline Jackson from *How Peter Cottontail Got His Name*, Wonder Books, 1957].
- 36 stories about Peter Rabbit.
- Wonder Read aloud books #2008.
- Also issued in a hard cover Gift Edition, 1958.

2. NATURE STORIES TO READ ALOUD — 1959

Thornton W. Burgess / Nature Stories / TO READ ALOUD / Illustrated by ADRIANNA MAZZA / [illus.] / WONDER BOOKS • NEW YORK

- c.1959.
- [2]-160p., many b&w illus., 20x13cm.
- green paper covers, yellow lettering, full-col. illus. bordered in yellow.
- 46 short stories about the Green Meadow and Green Forest creatures.
- Since the author's name appears at the head of the title, this book may also be known as "Thornton W. Burgess Nature Stories to Read Aloud."
- Wonder Read Aloud Books #2017.

3. MOTHER WEST WIND STORIES TO READ ALOUD — 1965

Mother West Wind / STORIES / TO READ ALOUD / By THORNTON W. BURGESS / Illustrated by SERGIO LEONE / [illus.] / WONDER BOOKS • NEW YORK / A Division of Grosset & Dunlap, Inc.

- c.1965. Published simultaneously in Canada.
- [4]-127p., many b&w illus., 20x13cm.
- blue paper covers, yellow and white lettering, full-col. illus. (from new G&D binding of about 1962).
- Contents consist of stories selected from the Mother West Wind Series.
    1. Bobby Coon and Reddy Fox Play Tricks (Story XII of *Old Mother West Wind*)
    2. Peter Rabbit Plays a Joke (Story IX of *Old Mother West Wind*)
    3. Johnny Chuck's Great Fight (Story VIII of *Mother West Wind's Children*)
    4. Reddy Fox Disobeys (Story IV of *Mother West Wind's Children*)
    5. Who Stole the Eggs of Mrs. Grouse (Story X of *Mother West Wind's Neighbors*)
    6. The Most Beautiful Thing in the World (Story VII of *Mother West Wind's Neighbors*)
    7. Striped Chipmunk Fools Peter Rabbit (Story XIII of *Mother West Wind's Animal Friends*)
    8. Jerry Muskrat's New House (Story XIV of *Mother West Wind's Animal Friends*)
    9. Spotty the Turtle Wins a Race (Story XVI of *Old Mother West Wind*)
    10. Grandfather Frog's Journey (Story XI of *Mother West Wind's Animal Friends*)
    11. Billy Mink's Swimming Party (Story VIII of *Old Mother West Wind*)
- Wonder Read Aloud Books #2052.

Dust wrapper of *Now I Remember*. Boston, Little, Brown, c.1960 by Thornton W. Burgess.

NOW I REMEMBER (1960)

Thornton W. Burgess / [decorative rule] / Now I Remember / AUTO-BIOGRAPHY OF / AN AMATEUR NATURALIST / [pub. logo] / Little, Brown and Company / BOSTON   TORONTO

- c.1960. The author wishes to thank *Cape Cod Compass* and *Natural History* for permission to use material which first appeared in their publications.

- [vi]-viii, [2]-338p., front. (a photograph of Burgess), 21x14 cm.

- black cloth on bds.; lettering on spine in yellow; green d.w. with lettering in white and yellow, flower design, and a photograph of Burgess on the back.

- ''To the memory of Alfred R. McIntyre, for whose helpful advice and guidance as my publisher through many years I am deeply indebted.''

- This book is Burgess's autobiography. The 35 chapters are his own reminiscences of his life, arranged roughly in chronological order. The topics include his childhood, his early struggles at a writing career, the art of his writing, his interests in nature, the banding of the world's last heath hen, his lecturing, correspondence, and many friends.

Dust wrapper of *The Burgess Book of Nature Lore*. Boston, Little, Brown, c.1965 by Thornton W. Burgess. Illus. by Robert Candy.

THE BURGESS BOOK OF NATURE LORE (1965)

The Burgess Book / of Nature Lore / Adventures of Tommy, Sue, and Sammy / with their Friends / of Meadow, Pool, and Forest / by / THORNTON W. BURGESS / Illustrated by Robert Candy / [pub. logo] / LITTLE, BROWN, AND COMPANY / BOSTON • TORONTO

- c.1965.

- [vi]-viii, [2]-255p., many b&w illus. incl. several full-page, 20x13cm.

- cloth on bds.; lettering stamped in black; yellow d.w. with illus. and lettering done in black, brown, and white.

- The 27 chapters contain miniature nature lessons interwoven with a plot. Sammy and Sue spend their summer vacation on a farm with their cousin Tommy Brown (whom Burgess fans will recognize as Farmer Brown's Boy). The Burgess animals are there but this time seen from a realistic, human point of view. Wise old Uncle Ben could be Burgess himself. Index pp.247-254.

- The book came out two months before Burgess's death.

- Also issued by Bonanza Books, a division of Crown Publishers, Inc., by arrangement with Little, Brown and Company.

Several publishers issued over 100 picture books and small paper booklets by Thornton W. Burgess. Shown are examples of the many varieties.

(Left) Dust wrapper of *Thornton Burgess Animal Stories*. New York, Platt & Munk, c.1940, 1942. Illus. by Harrison Cady.

(Right) Cover of *Wild Flowers We Know*. Racine, Wisconsin, Whitman Pub. Co., c.1929. Illus. by the Pitts Studios.

(Left) Centerfold by Harrison Cady from *Jumper the Hare Cannot Sleep*. (Right) Cover of *Jumper the Hare Cannot Sleep*. New York, John H. Eggers Co., c.1914, 1922, 1928. Illus. by Harrison Cady.

PICTURE BOOKS AND PAPER BOOKLETS
BY THORNTON W. BURGESS

Cover of *Burgess Animal Paint Book*. Akron, Saalfield Pub. Co., c.1925, reprinted 1978 by Thornton W. Burgess Society.

(Left) Cover of *Farmer Brown's Boy Becomes Curious*. Racine, Wisconsin, Whitman Pub. Co., c.1927, illus. c.1929. Illus by Nina R. Jordan.

(Right) Frontispiece by Phoebe Erickson from *Nature Almanac*. New York, Grosset & Dunlap, c.1949.

LITTLE ANIMAL STORIES
FOR LITTLE CHILDREN (1913)

Little Animal Stories for Little Children; Bedtime Stories for Little Folks. Illus.
by Leon Wolf. New York, John Martin's House, 1913. [30]p., col. illus.
incl. front., 28cm.

- brown paper on cardboard; lettering and illus. done in brown, green & blue;
green cloth spine; cover illus. by George Carlson; illus. end papers.
- (The Goody Gay Series) #4.

1916   Garden City, New York, John Martin's House. [32]p., illus. (part.
col.), 26cm.

- cardboard cover with illus. done in blue, yellow, & brown. (On cover: John Martin Jolly Book.)

THE JOY OF THE BEAUTIFUL PINE (1913)

The Joy of the Beautiful Pine: A Child's Christmas Story. A Christmas Story
Written Especially for the Children of Springfield. 1913. 6 l., photo.,
24x15cm., paper covers.

- Main feature in "Springfield's Christmas Tree: The Story of the Pageant of
1913," containing the program of the pageant, Burgess story, and a photo of a
pine tree.
- See also *Tales from the Storyteller's House,* p.90.

THIRTY-TWO BOOKS ORIGINALLY
COPYRIGHTED BY J. N. COLE, JR. (1914)

A.   J. N. Cole, Jr. of New York obtained the copyright on 32 books by Thornton W. Burgess in Dec. 1914. All have paper covers with the title page on the
front cover, [9]p. (or 12p. incl. covers), illus., 7x5½cm. The titles listed
alphabetically are:

1. Buster Bear Invites Old Mr. Toad to Dine
2. Busy Folks and Sleepy Folks
3. Danny Meadow Mouse Learns Something
4. The Digging Match
5. The Discontent of Peter Rabbit
6. The Feast at the Big Rock
7. Four Little Mice at School and Play
8. Fun With Farmer Brown's Boy

9. A Glad Time Made a Sad Time
10. Grandfather Frog Stays in the Smiling Pool
11. How Unc' Billy Possum Met Buster Bear
12. An Important Meeting at the Smiling Pool
13. Jack Frost Helps Paddy the Beaver
14. Jerry Muskrat Begins to Build
15. Jerry Muskrat is Laughed At
16. Jerry Muskrat Wins Respect
17. Johnny Chuck Loses His Temper
18. Jumper the Hare Cannot Sleep
19. Mr. Toad and Danny Meadow Mouse Take a Walk
20. Old Mr. Toad Gets His Stomach Full
21. Paddy the Beaver Gives Warning
22. Peter Rabbit Finds No One to Play With
23. Peter Rabbit Has Hard Work to Believe His Eyes
24. Peter Rabbit Introduces His Big Cousin
25. Peter Rabbit is Lonesome
26. Peter Rabbit Learns From Striped Chipmunk
27. Peter Rabbit Puts on Airs
28. The Stolen Eggs
29. The Strange Tracks in the Green Forest
30. Striped Chipmunk Has a Secret
31. Striped Chipmunk's Secret Joke
32. Unc' Billy Possum Has a Fright

These titles were first published by John H. Eggers, Co. of New York as miniature booklets and were issued in a variety of ways. Companies issued them with their names on the back for advertising purposes. The combined known titles of forms B, C, & D in this bibliography make up all 32 titles. Varieties B-F are all in miniature form. Of the known distributors, particularly the advertisers, each may have issued more titles than are listed, but those given are the known ones.

B. John H. Eggers issued a boxed set of 8 titles. The box has the cover-title of one of the stories pasted on it. Two box covers examined are "Mr. Toad and Danny Meadow Mouse Take a Walk and Other Stories," and "Four Little Mice at School and Play, and Other Stories." "John H. Eggers, New York" printed on box cover.

Each book has paper covers. (A list of books by Burgess is on the inside front cover, listing books through 1916.) Colored illus. [by Harrison Cady] in three colors on cover, 7cm., c.1914 J. N. Cole, c.1914 The Winthrop Press. (Other bibliographies give the publisher of the books as either John H. Eggers or The Winthrop Press. Egger's name comes from the box cover; The Winthrop Press from the verso of the title page of the books.) The titles are:

1. Danny Meadow Mouse Learns Something
2. The Feast at the Big Rock
3. A Glad Time Made a Sad Time
4. How Unc' Billy Possum Met Buster Bear
5. Jack Frost Helps Paddy the Beaver
6. Mr. Toad and Danny Meadow Mouse Take a Walk
7. Old Mr. Toad Gets His Stomach Full
8. Striped Chipmunk's Secret Joke

The Philadelphia *Bulletin* issued some in this same form with its name on the back cover. The known ones are 1, 3, 4, 6, & 8 of the "B" titles.

C. John H. Eggers Co. published 8 of the titles in 1917 in a box labeled "Little Animal Books" with a verse "Little Books of Animals, I'm sure you will enjoy, For they are the nicest things, For Any girl or boy!" The number 520 is on the lower left corner of the box, with "Rust Craft, Boston" on the side.

The books have paper covers with the title page on the front cover, 12p. incl. paper covers. (The same list of books by Burgess is on the inside front cover.) Colored illus. [by Harrison Cady] on front cover in three colors. Inside illus. [not by Cady] are in b&w on part of pages 3, 6, 7, and 11. 7cm., c.1917 John H. Eggers, N.Y. The titles are:

1. Busy Folks and Sleepy Folks
2. Four Little Mice at School and Play
3. An Important Meeting at the Smiling Pool
4. Johnny Chuck Loses His Temper
5. Paddy the Beaver Gives Warning
6. Peter Rabbit Introduces His Big Cousin
7. Peter Rabbit Learns From Striped Chipmunk
8. Striped Chipmunk Has a Secret

At least 6 of these titles were issued by the Anderson Candy Co. of Providence, Rhode Island for advertising purposes. Each has on the back cover "Home of Home-Made Candy, Anderson Candy Company, Providence, Rhode Island." The copyright is 1917 by John H. Eggers. The known books are 1, 2, 3, 4, 5, & 6 of the "C" titles.

The Philadelphia *Bulletin* also issued some titles in the "C" form. The known ones are 1, 3, 4, 5, 6, & 8.

D. 16 of the titles were copyrighted in 1922 by John H. Eggers and were issued in the same box described in "C." They have 12p. incl. paper covers, full-col. illus. by Harrison Cady on the cover and on part of pages 3, 6, 7, and a b&w one on p. 11. 7cm., c.1914, 1922. The titles are:

1. Buster Bear Invites Old Mr. Toad to Dine
2. The Digging Match
3. The Discontent of Peter Rabbit

4. Fun With Farmer Brown's Boy
5. Grandfather Frog Stays in the Smiling Pool
6. Jerry Muskrat Begins to Build
7. Jerry Muskrat is Laughed At
8. Jerry Muskrat Wins Respect
9. Jumper the Hare Cannot Sleep
10. Peter Rabbit Finds No One to Play With
11. Peter Rabbit Has Hard Work to Believe His Eyes
12. Peter Rabbit is Lonesome
13. Peter Rabbit Puts on Airs
14. The Stolen Eggs
15. The Strange Tracks in the Green Forest
16. Unc' Billy Possum Has a Fright

At least five of these titles were issued by the Philadelphia *Bulletin* for advertising purposes. On the back cover is printed "A new Bedtime Story similar to this one appears every evening in the *Bulletin*, Philadelphia." The known books are 1, 6, 7, 8, & 16 of the "D" titles and follow the "D" format.

The Courant of Hartford, Conn. also used books of the "D" form for advertising. The known titles are 2 and 6 of the "D" books.

Another book of the same form, "Fun With Farmer Brown's Boy," was issued attached to an Easter card by Rust Craft of Boston. (Perhaps other titles were issued also.)

The Great American Tea Co., New York issued all 16 titles with an advertisement on the back cover which says "You will find one of these little story books in every package of Golden Key Butter Crackers, Graham Wafers. . . ." etc.

The Besse System Co. of Meriden, Conn. issued at least one, "Peter Rabbit Has Hard Work to Believe His Eyes."

E.   8 titles appeared in a boxed set entitled "Eight Sleeptime Stories." [All illus. in col. by Harrison Cady], 12p. incl. paper covers, 7cm., c.1914, 1922. The titles include:

1. Busy Folks and Sleepy Folks
2. Fun With Farmer Brown's Boy
3. Jack Frost Helps Paddy the Beaver
4. Johnny Chuck Loses His Temper
5. Old Mr. Toad Gets His Stomach Full
6. Paddy the Beaver Gives Warning
7. Peter Rabbit Introduces His Big Cousin
8. Striped Chipmunk Has a Secret

F.   The Sterling Gum Company issued some of the titles with chewing gum. Copies examined are:

1. Jack Frost Helps Paddy the Beaver, [illus. by Harrison Cady], 12p., 7 cm., c.1914 J. N. Cole, c.1914 The Winthrop Press. The Sterling Gum Co.,

10th St. and Vernon Ave., N. Y., text printed over green illus. Of the two copies of this title examined, one had cover done in yellow and black; the other in yellow and blue.

2. Jerry Muskrat Begins to Build, same description as above except cover done in green & black.
3. Peter Rabbit Puts on Airs, cover done in tan and black.

G.   6 titles appeared in another size in 1922. The description of them is: Illus. by Harrison Cady. New York, John H. Eggers, c.1914, 1922. 16p. incl. paper covers, full-col. and b&w illus., 22cm. (Paging could also be called 12p. plus paper covers, or 13p. of text plus covers). Full-col. illus. on front cover, orange back cover, quote from *New York Times* and list of books in the series on inside back cover. The titles are:

1. Buster Bear Invites Old Mr. Toad to Dine
2. Grandfather Frog Stays in the Smiling Pool
3. Jerry Muskrat Wins Respect
4. Jumper the Hare Cannot Sleep
5. Peter Rabbit Puts on Airs
6. Unc' Billy Possum Has a Fright (spelled "Possom" on t.p., "Possum" on cover.)

There is a version of these with a black illus. on the back cover and the words "Stoll & Edwards Co., Inc. New York, Distributors." The Titcomb bibliography lists Stoll & Edwards as the publisher of the six titles. This may or may not have come from the statement on the back cover and a list of the 6 titles on the inside back cover.

In 1928, John H. Eggers Co. issued another edition of the six titles in the form: 6 l., 28cm., paper covers with col. illus. on front and back. Border illus. account for the larger size.

H.   In 1954, Burgess Associates obtained a copyright on titles which are the same or nearly the same as some of the original 32 titles. They are:

1. The Feast at the Big Rock
2. Peter Rabbit Learns From Striped Chipmunk
3. Reddy Fox Gets a Surprise; Peter Rabbit's Timid Cousin; No One Wants to Play [and others].

Items #1 and 2 are among the original 32 titles. It is unclear whether the titles in item #3 are each a part of one book or individual books. "Peter Rabbit's Timid Cousin" and "No One Wants to Play" may be the same as "Peter Rabbit Introduces His Big Cousin" and "Peter Rabbit Finds No One to Play With." These titles are listed only in the *Catalogue of Copyright Entries,* and no copies have been discovered.

LITTLE STORIES FOR BEDTIME (1915)

Little Stories for Bedtime. Illus. by Harrison Cady. New York, United Artists
Pub. Co., 1915. [25]p., illus. done in poster stamps, 32mo. (Stampkraft).

MY OWN BEDTIME STORY BOOK (1915)

My Own Bedtime Story Book. New York, The Globe, 1915 c. H. S. Tibbs.
[30]p., illus. done in poster stamps (sold separately), 10cm., paper covers,
12 stories.

HAPPY JACK SQUIRREL'S THRIFT CLUB (1918)

Happy Jack Squirrel's Thrift Club. Illus by Harrison Cady. Massachusetts War
Savings Committee, 1918. 13 l. incl. paper covers, b&w illus., 19cm.

- Peter Rabbit Becomes Disconsolate [first appeared in *Springfield Republican*,
  Mar. 21, 1918]
  Peter Rabbit Tries to Join the Club [*SR*, Mar. 22, 1918]
  Peter Rabbit Tries Hard to Be Thrifty [*SR* , Mar. 23, 1918]
  Peter Rabbit is Made Happy at Last [*SR,* Mar. 24, 1918]

- The Chairman of the Massachusetts War Savings Committee asked Burgess to
  write 5 stories to appear in local papers on the subjects of patriotism and thrift.
  Four of the stories, which were designed to help the sales of War Savings Bonds
  during World War I, are contained in the book.

PETER RABBIT BOOK (1920)

Peter Rabbit Book. Chicago, Chicago Evening American, 1920. 4 l., illus. after
Harrison Cady (illustrator not given), 20cm., paper covers.

- Contents: (1) Mrs. Peter is Very Mysterious, (2) Peter Receives a Fright and a
  Visitor, (3) Peter Cannot Believe What He Sees.

THIRTY-FOUR STORIES ON FOLDED CARDS (1920-1923)

1920
Peter Welcomes An Old Friend. 1920. 2.l., 1 col. illus., 9½x6½cm.
  (Story No. 1)
Johnny Chuck is Cross. 1920. 2 l., 1 col. illus., 9½x6½cm.
  (Story No. 2)
Johnny Chuck Loses His Fat. 1920. 2 l., 1 col. illus., 9½x6½cm.
  (Story No. 3)
Peter Discovers Johnny Chuck Far From Home. 1920. 2 l., 1 col. illus., 9½x6½cm.
  (Story No. 4)
An Unpleasant Surprise. 1920. 2 l., 1 col. illus., 9½x6½cm.
  (Story No. 5)

Peter Sees a New Johnny Chuck. 1920. 2 l., 1 col. illus., 9½x6½cm.
   (Story No. 6)
Peter Rabbit Has Great Respect. 1920. 2 l., 1 col. illus., 9½x6½cm.
   (Story No. 7)
Jimmy Skunk Proves a Friend Worth Having. 1920. 2 l., 1 col. illus., 9½x6½cm.
   (Story No. 8)
Old Man Coyote Takes His Time. 1920. 2 l., 1 col. illus., 9½x6½cm.
   (Story No. 9)
Old Man Coyote Suddenly Turns Very Polite. 1920. 2 l., 1 col. illus., 9½x6½cm.
   (Story No. 10)
The Gratefulness of Johnny Chuck. 1920. 2 l., 1 col. illus., 9½x6½cm.
   (Story No. 11)
Paddy the Beaver Does a Little Studying. 1920. 2 l., 1 col. illus., 9½x6½cm.
   (Story No. 12)
Paddy Makes Up His Mind. 1920. 2 l., 1 col. illus., 9½x6½cm.
   (Story No. 13)
Peter is Filled With Admiration. 1920. 2 l., 1 col. illus., 9½x6½cm.
   (Story No. 14)
Peter Gets a Lesson in Logging. 1920. 2 l., 1 col. illus., 9½x6½cm.
   (Story No. 15)
The Queer Case of Buster Bear. 1920. 2 l., 1 col. illus., 9½x6½cm.
   (Story No. 16)

1922
Unc' Billy Possum is Peevish. 1922. 2 l., 1 col. illus., 9½x6½cm.
• 1923   (Copyrighted as Story No. 17)
Peter Rabbit Tries to Sleep. 1922. 2 l., 1 col. illus., 9½x6½cm.
• 1923   (Copyrighted as Story No. 18)
Grandfather Frog Explains How He Breathes. 1922. 2 l., 1 col. illus., 9½x6½cm.
Peter Jumps For His Life. 1922. 2 l., 1 col. illus., 9½x6½cm.
Mrs. Peter is Very Mysterious. 1922. 2 l., 1 col. illus., 9½x6½cm.
• 1923   (Copyrighted as Story No. 21)
Little Mrs. Peter's Surprise. 1922. 2 l., 1 col. illus., 9½x6½cm.
• 1923   (Copyrighted as Story No. 22)
Happy Jack Gets Busy. 1922. 2 l., 1 col. illus., 9½x6½cm.
• 1923   (Copyrighted as Story No. 23)
Hooty and Mrs. Hooty Go House Hunting. 1922. 2 l., 1 col. illus., 9½x6½cm.
• 1923   (Copyrighted as Story No. 24)
Jenny Wren Makes a Discovery. 1922. 2 l., 1 col. illus., 9½x6½cm.
• 1923   (Copyrighted as Story No. 25)
Jenny and Mr. Wren Argue. 1922. 2 l., 1 col. illus., 9½x6½cm.
• 1923   (Copyrighted as Story No. 26)
A Scandal in the Jay Family. 1922. 2 l., 1 col. illus., 9½x6½cm.
• 1923   (Copyrighted as Story No 27)
Why Danny Meadow Mouse Tried to Sing. 1922. 2 l., 1 col. illus., 9½x6½cm.
• 1923   (Copyrighted as Story No. 28)

The Bashful Hero. 1922. 2 l., 1 col. illus., 9½x6½cm.
* 1923   (Copyrighted as Story No. 29)
The Broken Nap. 1922. 2 l., 1 col. illus., 9½x6½cm.
* 1923   (Copyrighted as Story No. 30)
Buster Bear Plays a Trick. 1922. 2 l., 1 col. illus., 9½x6½cm.
* 1923   (Copyrighted as Story No. 31)
Reddy Fox Does a Mean Thing. 1922. 2 l., 1 col. illus., 9½x6½cm.
* 1923   (Copyrighted as Story No. 32)

1923
Paddy the Beaver is Ready. 1923. 2 l., 1 col. illus., 9½x6½cm.
What Happened When Farmer Brown's Boy Jumped. 1923. 2 l., 1 col. illus.,
    9½x6½cm.

No publisher is given on these paper booklets. Thornton W. Burgess obtained the copyright on 16 of the titles in 1920 and 16 more in 1922. In 1923, fourteen of the 1922 titles were recopyrighted and given numbers. The two that were not listed in the *Catalogue of Copyright Entries* of 1923 were probably numbers 19 and 20, since no book in that list had those numbers. Two additional titles, also unnumbered, appeared only in the 1923 copyright list, making a total of thirty-four titles. One of the stories, "Mrs. Peter is Very Mysterious," appears in *Peter Rabbit Book* (see p.113). "Little Mrs. Peter's Surprise" may be the same as "Peter Receives a Fright and a Visitor" in *Peter Rabbit Book*.

One copy examined, "A Scandal in the Jay Family," contains an advertisement for "Peter Rabbit Crackers."

JOHN H. EGGERS CO.
— SET OF SIX BOOKS (1924)

Baby Possum's Queer Voyage. Illus. by Harrison Cady. New York, John H. Eggers, 1924. 8 l. incl. paper covers, full-col. illus., 18cm.
1928   New York, Stoll & Edwards, [1928]. [5]-29p., full-col. illus. and b&w & pink illus., 20cm., paper on bd. covers with full-col. illus.
* p.l. is p. [3-4], 2nd l. is p. [5]-6. c.1912 — J.G. Lloyd [for the newspaper story], c.1927 — The Associated Newspapers, illus. c.1927 — John H. Eggers Co., Inc.,N.Y.
* Also issued by Whitman Pub. Co., Racine, Wis.
Digger the Badger Decides to Stay. Illus. by Harrison Cady. New York, John H. Eggers, 1924. 8 l. incl. paper covers, full-col. illus., 18cm.

- Text is the same as "How Digger the Badger Came to the Green Meadows," story #XI in *Mother West Wind's Neighbors*, 1913.

1928   New York, Stoll & Edwards, [1928]. [5]-29p., full-col. illus. and b&w & pink illus., 20cm., paper on bd. covers with full col. illus.

- p.l. is p. [3-4], 2nd l. is p. [5]-6. c.1912 — J. G. Lloyd, c.1927 — The Associated Newspapers, illus. c.1927 — John H. Eggers Co., Inc., N.Y.

- Also issued by Whitman Pub. Co., Racine, Wis.

Grandfather Frog Gets a Ride. Illus. by Harrison Cady. New York, John H. Eggers, 1924. 8 l. incl. paper covers, full-col. illus., 18cm.

1928   New York, Stoll & Edwards, [1928]. [5]-29p., full-col. illus., and b&w & pink illus., 20cm., paper on bd. covers with full-col. illus.

- p.l. is p. [3-4], 2nd l. is p. [5]-6. c. 1912 — J. G. Lloyd, c.1927 — The Associated Newspapers, illus. c.1927 — John H. Eggers Co., Inc., N.Y.

- Also issued by Whitman Pub. Co., Racine Wis.

A Great Joke on Jimmy Skunk. Illus. by Harrison Cady. New York, John H. Eggers, 1924. 8 l. incl. paper covers, full-col. illus., 18cm.

1928   New York, Stoll & Edwards, [1928]. [6]-29p., full-col. illus. and b&w & pink illus., 20cm., paper on bd. covers with full-col. illus.

- p.l. is p. [3-4], 2nd l. is p. [5-6]. c. 1912 — J. G. Lloyd, c.1927 — The Associated Newspapers, illus. c.1927 — John H. Eggers Co., Inc., N.Y.

- Also issued by Whitman Pub. Co., Racine, Wis.

Happy Jack Squirrel Helps Unc' Billy. Illus. by Harrison Cady. New York, John H. Eggers, 1924. 8 l. incl. paper covers, full-col. illus., 18cm.

- Text is the same as Chapter XXIV of *The Adventures of Unc' Billy Possum*, 1914.

1928   New York, Stoll & Edwards, [1928]. [5]-29p., full-col. illus. and b&w & pink illus., 20cm., paper on bd. covers with full-col. illus.

- p.l. is p. [3-4], 2nd l. is p. [5]-6. c.1913 — J. G. Lloyd, c.1927 — The Associated Newspapers, illus. c.1927 — John H. Eggers Co., Inc., N.Y.

- Also issued by Whitman Pub. Co., Racine, Wis.

The Neatness of Bobby Coon. Illus. by Harrison Cady. New York, John H. Eggers, 1924. 8 l. incl. paper covers, full-col. illus., 18cm.

1928   New York, Stoll & Edwards, [1928]. [5]-29p., full-col. illus. and b&w & pink illus., 20cm., paper on bd. covers with full-col. illus.

- p.l. is p. [3-4], 2nd l. is p. [5]-6. c.1912 — J.G. Lloyd, c.1927 — The Associated Newspapers, illus. c.1927 — John H. Eggers Co., Inc., N.Y.

- Also issued by Whitman Pub. Co., Racine, Wis.

Each book in the Stoll & Edwards and Whitman editions came in a colored box.

SAALFIELD PUB. CO. — SIX BOOKS (1925)

Animal Folk. Illus. by Harrison Cady. Akron, Saalfield Pub. Co., 1925.

Burgess Animal Paint Book. Verses by Thornton W. Burgess. Illus. by Harrison Cady. Akron, Saalfield Pub. Co., 1925. 12 l., col. and b&w illus., 26x36cm., paper covers with col. illus.

1978   Reprinted by Thornton W. Burgess Society, Sandwich, Mass. Printed by Sullwold Pub., Inc. Taunton, Mass. 6 l., col. model illus. exchanged for new b&w illus., black border on covers.

Friendly Animals. Illus. by Harrison Cady. Akron, Saalfield Pub. Co., 1925.

Peter Cottontail's Own Paint Book. Verses by Thornton W. Burgess. Drawings by Harrison Cady. Akron, Saalfield Pub. Co., 1925.

Picture Book. Illus. by Harrison Cady. Akron, Saalfield Pub. Co., 1925.

Animal Pictures. Illus. by Harrison Cady. New York & Akron, Saalfield Pub. Co., 1925. [6] double leaves, 10 full-col. illus., 21cm.

- Printed on muslin. Author's name at head of title. Verse with each picture.

JOHN H. EGGERS
— SET OF SIX BOOKS (1928)

Baby Possum Has a Scare. Illus. by Harrison Cady. New York, John H. Eggers, 1928. 6 l. incl. paper covers, full-col. illus. [from *Baby Possum's Queer Voyage,* John H. Eggers, 1924], 18cm.

- stiff paper leaves bordered with red & blue Cady figures.

Bowser The Hound Meets His Match. Illus. by Harrison Cady. New York, John H. Eggers, 1928. 6 l. incl. paper covers, full-col. illus. [from *Digger the Badger Decides to Stay,* John H. Eggers, 1924], 18cm.

- stiff paper leaves bordered with blue & yellow Cady figures.

Grandfather Frog Fools Farmer Brown's Boy. Illus. by Harrison Cady. New York, John H. Eggers, 1928. 6 l. incl. paper covers, full-col. illus., 18cm.

- stiff paper leaves bordered with red & yellow Cady figures.

Peter Rabbit Learns to Use His New Coat. Illus. by Harrison Cady. New York, John H. Eggers, 1928. 6 l. incl. paper covers, full-col. illus. [from *A Great Joke on Jimmy Skunk,* John H. Eggers, 1924], 18cm.

- stiff paper leaves bordered with blue & yellow Cady figures.

Happy Jack Squirrel's Bright Idea. Illus. by Harrison Cady. New York, John H. Eggers, 1928. 6 l. incl. paper covers, full-col. illus. [from *Happy Jack Squirrel Helps Unc' Billy*, John H. Eggers, 1924], 18cm.
* stiff paper leaves bordered with blue & black Cady figures.

Bobby Coon Has a Good Time. Illus. by Harrison Cady. New York, John H. Eggers, 1928. 6 l. incl. paper covers, full-col. illus. [from *The Neatness of Bobby Coon*, John H. Eggers, 1924], 18cm.
* stiff paper leaves bordered with blue & red Cady figures.

The text of all 6 books c.1912 — J. G. Lloyd. Illus. c.1928 John H. Eggers. These books were also issued for advertising purposes. The I. Miller Shoe Co. of New York issued at least three with its advertisement on the back cover. They are *Bowser the Hound Meets His Match*, *Grandfather Frog Fools Farmer Brown's Boy*, and *Peter Rabbit Learns to Use His New Coat*.

CUBBY BEAR BOOKS (1929)

A Frightened Baby. Illus. by Nina R. Jordan. Racine, Wisconsin, Whitman Pub. Co., 1929. [24]p., full-col. illus., 11x13cm., paper on bd. covers.
* Also issued in 11x12cm. size, folded cardboard covers.

Farmer Brown's Boy Becomes Curious. Illus. by Nina R. Jordan. Racine, Wisconsin, Whitman Pub. Co., 1929. [24]p., full-col. illus., 11x13cm., paper on bd. covers.
* Also issued in 11x12cm. size, folded cardboard covers.

What Farmer Brown's Boy Did. Illus. by Nina R. Jordan. Racine, Wisconsin, Whitman Pub. Co., 1929. [24]p., full-col. illus. 11x13cm., paper on bd. covers.
* Also issued in 11x12cm. size, folded cardboard covers.

Cubby Bear Has a Mind of His Own. Illus. by Nina R. Jordan. Racine, Wisconsin, Whitman Pub. Co., 1929. [24]p., full-col. illus., 11x13cm., paper on bd. covers.
* Cover title is "Cubby Bear Had a Mind of His Own."
* Also issued in 11x12cm. size, folded cardboard covers.

An Imp of Mischief. Illus. by Nina R. Jordan. Racine, Wisconsin, Whitman Pub. Co., 1929. [24]p., full-col. illus., 11x13cm., paper on bd. covers.

Cubby in Mother Brown's Pantry. Illus. by Nina R. Jordan. Racine, Wisconsin, Whitman Pub. Co., 1929. [24]p., full-col. illus., 11x13cm., paper on bd. covers.

- Also issued in 11x12cm. size, folded cardboard covers.

A Woe-Begone Little Bear. Illus. by Nina R. Jordan. Racine, Wisconsin, Whitman Pub. Co., 1929. [24]p., full-col. illus., 11x13cm., paper on bd. covers.

- Also issued in 11x12cm. size, folded cardboard covers.

Cubby Gets a Bath. Illus. by Nina R. Jordan. Racine, Wisconsin, Whitman Pub. Co., 1929. [24]p., full-col. illus., 11x13cm., paper on bd. covers.

- Also issued in 11x12cm. size, folded cardboard covers.

Milk and Honey. Illus. by Nina R. Jordan. Racine, Wisconsin, Whitman Pub. Co., 1929. [24]p., full-col. illus., 11x13cm., paper on bd. covers.

Cubby Finds an Open Door. Illus. by Nina R. Jordan. Racine, Wisconsin, Whitman Pub. Co., 1929. [24]p., full-col. illus., 11x13cm., paper on bd. covers.

- Also issued in 11x12cm. size, folded cardboard covers.

The inside front covers of all the books contain a note printed in script to the readers from the author. The inside back covers contain a list of the Cubby Bear Books (10 books in the larger size, 8 in the smaller.) The larger books were issued with col. dust wrappers. The smaller books were issued in boxed sets, "2 books in a box."

The text of the 10 books was copyrighted in 1927 when the stories ran in Burgess's daily Bedtime Stories newspaper column from Aug. 16-Sept. 9, 1927.

WILD FLOWERS WE KNOW
and WILD FLOWERS WE SHOULD KNOW (1929)

Wild Flowers We Know. Illus. by the Pitts Studios. Racine, Wisconsin, Whitman Pub. Co., 1929. 10 l. incl. paper covers, full-col. illus., 31cm.

- Text on inside of front and back covers.

Wild Flowers We Should Know. Illus. by the Pitts Studios. Racine, Wisconsin, Whitman Pub. Co., 1929. 10 l. incl. paper covers. full-col. illus., 31cm.

- Text on inside of front and back covers.

WHITMAN PUB. CO.
— SET OF 6 BOOKS (1929-1923)

Little Joe Otter's Slide. Racine, Wisconsin, Whitman Pub. Co., 1929. 38p., b&w illus., 9cm., paper covers.

Betty Bear's Lesson. Racine, Wisconsin, Whitman Pub. Co., 1930. 38p., b&w illus., 9cm., paper covers.

Unc' Billy Gets Even. Racine, Wisconsin, Whitman Pub. Co., 1930. 39p., b&w illus., 9cm., paper covers.

Whitefoot's Secret. Racine, Wisconsin, Whitman Pub. Co., 1930. 38p., b&w illus., 9 cm., paper covers.

Jimmy Skunk's Justice. Racine, Wisconsin, Whitman Pub. Co., 1933. 39p., b&w illus., 9cm., paper covers.

Peter Rabbit's Carrots. Racine, Wisconsin, Whitman Pub. Co., 1933. 38p., b&w illus., 9cm., paper covers.

The books were issued as a boxed set "6 Wee Little Books by Thornton W. Burgess." The illustrator's name isn't given.

WAH-WAH-TAYSEE AND THE JAY'S WING (1935)

Wah-Wah-Taysee and the Jay's Wing. Illus. by Jack Canning. Pittsfield, Mass., Mohawk Beverages, 1935. 4 l. incl. paper covers, illus., 23cm.

MOTHER NATURE'S
SONG AND STORY BOOK (1938)

Mother Nature's Song and Story Book. By Thornton W. Burgess and Rebecca Richards. [Illus. by Henry H. Johnson and Lemuel Palmer.] Boston, John Worley Co., 1938. 15p., illus. and music, 31cm., paper covers.

- Stories and accompanying songs:
  Welcome Robin's Long Journey — Welcome Robin
  A Queer Reason for Being Glad — Peter Rabbit
  A Funny Fiddler's Funny Elbow — Little Black Cricket
  A Homely Fellow Sings His Joy — Old Mr. Toad
  Bob White's Little Joke — Bob White
  Why the Chorus Stopped — The Smiling Pool

- Burgess wrote the stories and song lyrics. Rebecca Richards wrote the music. The book contains a map of Burgess settings.

PLATT & MUNK — SET OF 8 BOOKS (1940)

Bobby Coon's Mistake. Illus. by Harrison Cady. [New York], Platt & Munk, 1940. [12]p. incl. paper covers, full-col. and b&w illus., 21cm.

- Full-col. illus. on front cover, b&w illus. and poem "Bobby Coon" on back cover.

1961   Reissued under title "Bobby Coon's Surprise," front cover with white border and reduced col. illus., poem deleted from back cover.

The Three Little Bears. Illus. by Harrison Cady. [New York], Platt & Munk, 1940. [12]p. incl. paper covers, full-col. and b&w illus., 21cm.

- Full-col. illus. on front cover, b&w illus. and poem "Little Bears" on back cover.

1961   Reissued under title "A Bear Scare," front cover with white border and reduced col. illus., poem deleted from back cover.

Peter Rabbit Proves a Friend. Illus. by Harrison Cady. [New York], Platt & Munk, 1940. [12]p. incl. paper covers, full-col. and b&w illus., 21cm.

- Full-col. illus. on front cover, b&w illus. and poem "Old Mr. Toad" on back cover.

1961   Reissued under title "Peter Rabbit Goes Scouting," front cover with white border and reduced col. illus., poem deleted from back cover.

Reddy Fox's Sudden Engagement. Illus. by Harrison Cady. [New York], Platt & Munk, 1940. [12]p. incl. paper covers, full-col. and b&w illus., 21cm.

- Full-col. illus. on front cover, b&w illus. and poem "Reddy Fox" on back cover.

1961   Reissued under title "Reddy Fox Leaves in a Hurry," front cover with white border and reduced col. illus., poem deleted from back cover.

Paddy's Surprise Visitor. Illus. by Harrison Cady. [New York], Platt & Munk, 1940. [12]p. incl. paper covers, full-col. and b&w illus., 21cm.

- Full-col. illus. on front cover, b&w illus. and poem "Paddy the Beaver" on back cover.

1961   Reissued under title "Paddy the Beaver's Visitor," front cover with white border and reduced col. illus., poem deleted from back cover.

A Merry Coasting Party. Illus. by Harrison Cady. [New York], Platt & Munk, 1940. [12]p. incl. paper covers, full-col. and b&w illus., 21cm.

- Full-col. illus. on front cover, b&w illus. and poem "Little Joe Otter" on back cover.

1961   Reissued under title "Fun at the Queer Trail," front cover with white border and reduced col. illus., poem deleted from back cover.

Young Flash the Deer. Illus. by Harrison Cady. [New York], Platt & Munk, 1940. [12]p. incl. paper covers, full-col. and b&w illus., 21cm.

  - Full-col. illus. on front cover, b&w illus. and poem "Young Flash the Deer" on back cover.

1961   Reissued under title "Flash the Young Deer," front cover with white border and reduced illus., poem deleted from back cover.

A Robber Meets His Match. Illus. by Harrison Cady. [New York], Platt & Munk, 1940. [12]p. incl. paper covers, full-col. and b&w illus., 21cm.

  - Full-col. illus. on front cover, b&w illus. and poem "Robber the Rat" on back cover.

1961   Reissued under title "Robber the Rat Loses Out," front cover with white border and reduced illus., poem deleted from back cover.

The original 8 books were issued as a boxed set "Thornton Burgess Animal Library." The yellow and blue box cover was illustrated by Harrison Cady. [New York], Platt & Munk.

Two more boxes have been examined which may or may not have contained linenlike versions of the books. Their descriptions are:

"Bedtime Nature Library." "8 Linenlike books in this box." No. 3700. c.1940 The Platt & Munk Co., red paper covering on box cover with col. illus. by Harrison Cady. 22x19cm.

"In the Fields Nature Stories." "4 Linenlike books in this box." No. 2595A. c.1940 The Platt & Munk Co., yellow paper covering on box cover with col. illus. by Harrison Cady. 22x19cm.

The 8 books were also issued in 1952 in a boxed set "Animal Story Library" together with 8 "Uncle Wiggily" books of the same size by Howard R. Garis and illustrated by George Carlson. [New York], Platt & Munk. The black paper covered box was illustrated with color animal figures and lettering, and numbered 3637.

*1942   Animal Stories. Illus. by Harrison Cady. New York, Platt & Munk, 1942. [96]p., full-col. and b&w illus., 21cm.

  - orange cloth on bds., lettering and illus. stamped in black, full-col. d.w. with illus. from cover of "Bobby Coon's Mistake," illus. end papers.
  - contains the eight stories in the order listed above. The covers of the original books appear as illustrations without the lettering.
  - Since the author's name appears at the head of the title, the book is sometimes known as "Thornton Burgess Animal Stories."

*1961   The Animal World of Thornton W. Burgess. Illus. by Harrison Cady.
New York, Platt & Munk, 1961. [96]p., full-col. and b&w illus., 21cm.

  • green paper on bds., lettering and illus. stamped in dark green, full-col. d.w.
    with illus. from cover of "Young Flash the Deer."
  • contains the eight stories under the 1961 titles and in a different order. The
    covers of the individual books appear as illustrations without the lettering and
    poems. The story titles are:
  1. Flash the Young Deer
  2. Peter Rabbit Goes Scouting
  3. Fun at the Queer Trail
  4. Bobby Coon's Surprise
  5. Robber the Rat Loses Out
  6. Reddy Fox Leaves in a Hurry
  7. Paddy the Beaver's Visitor
  8. A Bear Scare

THE BURGESS STORY MAGAZINE (1940)

The Burgess Story Magazine. No. 1. Illus. by Harrison Cady. New York,
Burgess-Gates Co., 1940. 64p., illus., 24x17cm., paper covers with col.
illus.

  • Thornton W. Burgess was the president of the Burgess-Gates Co., and Moody B.
    Gates was the vice-president and treasurer. Since this is the only number issued,
    it is included here as a paper booklet. It contains 24 stories and 10 Mother
    Nature's News Items.

THE LITTLE BURGESS BIRD BOOK FOR CHILDREN and
THE LITTLE BURGESS ANIMAL BOOK FOR CHILDREN
(1941)

The Little Burgess Bird Book for Children. Illus. by Louis Agassiz Fuertes.
Chicago, Rand McNally & Co., 1941. 64p., full-col. and b&w illus.,
16cm., paper on bd. covers.

  • Illustrations first appeared in *The Burgess Bird Book for Children*. Boston, Little,
    Brown, 1919.

The Little Burgess Animal Book for Children. Illus. by Louis Agassiz Fuertes.
Chicago, Rand McNally & Co., 1941. 64p., full-col. and b&w illus.,
16cm., paper on bd. covers.

  • Illustrations first appeared in *The Burgess Animal Book for Children*. Boston,
    Little, Brown, 1920.

LITTLE COLOR CLASSICS (1941-1942)

Little Pete's Adventure. Illus. by Harrison Cady. Springfield, Mass.,
McLoughlin Bros., 1941. [60]p. incl. col. front., col. and b&w illus.,
17cm., paper on bd. covers.

  • (Little Color Classics, #891.)

Little Chuck's Adventure. Illus. by Harrison Cady. Springfield, Mass.,
McLoughlin Bros., 1942. [60]p. incl. col. front., col. and b&w illus.,
17cm., paper on bd. covers.

  • (Little Color Classics, #897.)

Little Red's Adventure. Illus. by Harrison Cady. Springfield, Mass.,
McLoughlin Bros., 1942. [60]p. incl. col. front., col. and b&w illus.,
17cm., paper on bd. covers.

  • (Little Color Classics, #892.)

WHY PETER RABBIT'S EARS ARE LONG (1942)

Why Peter Rabbit's Ears Are Long and Three Other Stories. Drawings by Mary
and Wallace Stover after George F. Kerr. Sandusky, Ohio, The American
Crayon Co., 1944. [24]p. illus. in black and yellow, 28cm., paper covers.

  • (A Mary Perks Book.)

  • Why Peter Rabbit's Ears Are Long [Story III of *Mother West Wind's Children*]
    Striped Chipmunk's Pockets [Story V of *Mother West Wind's Children*]
    Reddy Fox Barks at the Moon [Story IV, ''Reddy Fox Disobeys'' in *Mother West
        Wind's Children*]
    How Reddy Fox Was Surprised [Story III of *Old Mother West Wind*]

  • The last three pages, not by Burgess, contain familiar children's prayers.

BABY ANIMAL STORIES and NATURE ALMANAC (1949)

Baby Animal Stories. Illus. by Phoebe Erickson. New York, Grosset & Dunlap,
1949. [29]p., full-col. and b&w illus., 29cm.

  • plastic coated green paper on bds. with yellow and white lettering, full-col.
    illus., End papers are a map ''Burgessville, U.S.A.''

Nature Almanac. Illus. by Phoebe Erickson. New York, Grosset & Dunlap,
1949. [29]p., full-col. and b&w illus., 29cm.

  • plastic coated green paper on bds., with black and green lettering, full-col. illus.,
    illus. end papers.

*1955   Stories Around the Year. Illus. by Phoebe Erickson. New York,
Grosset & Dunlap, 1955. 14 l., full-col. and b&w illus., 34cm.

  • plastic coated red paper on bds. with full-col. illus. End papers are the map
    "Burgessville, U.S.A."

  • (Big Treasure Books.) (Also issued in Dandelion Library format.)

  • The material, arranged by the seasons of the year, was taken from the author's
    and artist's books *Baby Animal Stories* and *Nature Almanac*.

A THORNTON BURGESS PICTURE STORY BOOK (1950)

A Thornton Burgess Picture Story Book. Illus. by Nino Carbe. Garden City,
N.Y., Garden City Publishing, 1950. [48]p., col. illus., 30cm., paper on
bds. with full-col. cover illus.

  • Contents: (1) Unc' Billy Possum, (2) Peter Rabbit's Prank, (3) What Mr. Toad
    Did With His Old Suit, (4) Everybody Lends Jerry Muskrat a Hand, (5) Reddy
    Fox Gets a Bath.

  • This book was published without Burgess's knowledge, the copyright on the
    stories having expired. The stories appeared originally in Burgess's newspaper
    Bedtime Stories and in *John Martin's Book: A Magazine for Little Children*,
    1912-1914. (See individual books below.)

*1953   The five stories were also published as individual picture books,
copyrighted by James and Jonathan, Inc.:

Unc' Billy Possum. Illus. by Nino Carbe. New York and Kenosha, Wisconsin,
Samuel Lowe Co., 1953. [24]p., col. and b&w illus., 20cm., cardboard
covers with full-col. illus., polka dot spine.

  • Appeared in *John Martin's Book* (Dec. 1912).

Peter Rabbit's Prank. Illus. by Nino Carbe. New York and Kenosha,
Wisconsin, Samuel Lowe Co., 1953. [24]p., col. and b&w illus., 20cm.,
cardboard covers with full-col. illus., polka dot spine. #805725.

  • Appeared in *John Martin's Book* (Jan. 1914).

What Mr. Toad Did With His Old Suit. Illus. by Nino Carbe. New York and
Kenosha, Wisconsin, Samuel Lowe Co., 1953. [24]p., col. and b&w illus.,
20cm., cardboard covers with full-col. illus., polka dot spine. #805925.

  • Appeared as the newspaper Bedtime Story of Mar. 21, 1912 and in *John Martin's
    Book* (May 1913).

Everybody Lends Jerry Muskrat a Hand. Illus. by Nino Carbe. New York and
Kenosha, Wisconsin, Samuel Lowe Co., 1953. [24]p., col. and b&w illus.,
20cm., cardboard covers with full-col. illus., polka dot spine. #805625.

- Appeared as the newspaper Bedtime Story of Aug. 12, 1912 and in *John Martin's Book* (Mar. 1913).

Reddy Fox Takes a Bath. Illus. by Nino Carbe. New York and Kenosha, Wisconsin, Samuel Lowe Co., 1953. [24]p., col. and b&w illus., 20cm., cardboard covers with full-col. illus., polka dot spine. #805825.

- Appeared in John Martin's Book (Mar. 1914).

*1954   Story Book. Illus. by Nino Carbe. Garden City, New York, Garden City Books, 1954.

THE THORNTON W. BURGESS STORY COLORING BOOK
(1954)

The Thornton W. Burgess Story Coloring Book; Favorite Stories and Favorite Pictures to Color by America's Leading Nature Story Teller. New York, Treasure Books (a division of Grosset & Dunlap), 1954.

WONDER BOOKS (1954-1957)

Peter Rabbit and Reddy Fox. Illus. by Mary and Carl Hauge. New York, Wonder Books (a division of Grosset & Dunlap), 1954. [20]p., col. illus., 21cm.

- plastic coated blue paper on bds., full-col. illus., front end paper is an extension of title page illus.
- (Wonder Books, #611).
- Also issued under title "Peter Cottontail and Reddy Fox," 1974, plastic coated paper on bds., new cover illus. (Wonder Books, #843).

The Littlest Christmas Tree. Illus. by Mary and Carl Hauge. New York, Wonder Books, 1954. [20]p., col. illus., front end paper is an extension of title page.

- (Wonder Books, #625.)

Little Peter Cottontail. Illus. by Phoebe Erickson. New York, Wonder Books, 1956. [20]p., col. illus., 21cm.

- plastic coated paper on bds., in three color varieties (pink, green, and yellow), all have same col. illus.
- (Wonder Books, #641).

How Peter Cottontail Got His Name; Adapted and Abridged from The Adventures of Peter Cottontail. Illus. by Pauline Jackson, New York, Wonder Books, 1957. [20]p., col. illus., 21cm.

- plastic coated paper on bds. with full-col. illus., front end paper is an extension of title page illus.
- (Wonder Books, #668.)
- This story is adapted and abridged from Chapters I & II of *The Adventures of Peter Cottontail* by Thornton W. Burgess. Boston, Little, Brown, 1914.

THE MILLION LITTLE SUNBEAMS (1963)

The Million Little Sunbeams. With an illus. by Harrison Cady. Toledo, Six Oaks Press, 1963. 3 l., illus., 7cm., yellow paper covers with illus. of the sun.

- Burgess first read this story publicly at a meeting of the Boston Author's Club. A story "A Million Little Sunbeams" appeared in John Martin's Book (June 1914). The story was printed as Burgess's 10,000th newspaper Nature Story on Jan. 29, 1944. Paul W. Kieser of Toledo, Ohio (formerly of Longmeadow, Mass.) had this miniature book privately published in 1963 as a tribute to his friend Burgess as he approached his 90th birthday. Kieser included a book in each of his 1963 Christmas cards. Burgess considered the piece to be one of the best things he had ever written.

APPENDIX

NOTES ON BOOKS APPEARING IN BURGESS'S DAILY NEWSPAPER STORIES

Thornton W. Burgess wrote over 15,000 Bedtime Stories for newspaper syndication. From the first story appearing in February, 1912, until 1920, he wrote for the Associated Newspapers Syndicate (including *The New York Globe* and *The Boston Globe*). From 1920 until the end of his newspaper career in the late 50's, he wrote for the *New York Herald Tribune* Syndicate. During the entire time the stories appeared under several headings including "Bedtime Stories," "Little Bedtime Stories," "Little Stories for Bedtime," and "Nature Stories." This daily column provided the text for many of the books, a day's story generally being equal to a chapter. During the compilation of this bibliography, note has been made of the dates that several book texts and portions of texts appeared. Exhaustive research would reveal even more of the books and short stories first appearing in the newspapers. Without comment on how Burgess edited the stories for the books, the titles and the dates they appeared are listed here. Chapters are indicated when the stories did not appear in consecutive order.

Bedtime Story-Books

The Adventures of Reddy Fox: Apr. 16-18, 1912 (Ch. I-III), Aug. 22-Sept. 21, 1912 (Ch. IV-XXVI).

The Adventures of Johnny Chuck: Mar. 11-12, 1913 (Ch. I-II), Mar. 20-21, 1913 (Ch. III-IV), Mar. 25-Apr. 16, 1913 (Ch. V-XXIV).

The Adventures of Peter Cottontail: May 14-17, 1913 (Ch. I-III), Mar. 15-17, 1912 (Ch. IV-VI), June 28-July 10,1912 (Ch. VII-XVII), Dec. 24, 1912-Jan. 2, 1913 (Ch. XVIII-XXVI).

The Adventures of Unc' Billy Possum: May 22-27, 1912 (Ch. I-V), June 4-12, 1912 (Ch. VI-XII), Feb. 17-Mar. 3, 1913 (Ch. XIII-XXV).

The Adventures of Mr. Mocker: Oct. 15-Nov. 14, 1912.

The Adventures of Jerry Muskrat: May 15-18, 1912 (Ch. I-III), Mar. 2-5, 1912 (Ch. IV-VI), May 19-June 9, 1913 (Ch. VII-XXV).

The Adventures of Danny Meadow Mouse: Apr. 20-22, 1912 (Ch. I-II), Jan. 24-Feb. 12, 1913 (Ch. III-XIX), Sept. 27-Oct. 2, 1913 (Ch. XX-XXIV).

The Adventures of Grandfather Frog: Oct. 4-31, 1913.

The Adventures of Chatterer the Red Squirrel: Dec. 10-20, 1913 (Ch. I-VII), Jan. 19-Feb. 9, 1914 (Ch. VIII-XXIII).

The Adventures of Sammy Jay: Mar. 4-8, 1913 (Ch. I-V), Dec. 27, 1913-Jan. 17, 1914 (Ch. VII-XXIV).

The Adventures of Buster Bear: May 27-June 13, 1914 (Ch. I-XVI), Sept. 2-14, 1914 (Ch. XVII-XXIII).

The Adventures of Old Mr. Toad: Apr. 6-Apr. 22, 1915 (Ch. I-XV), Mar. 26-28, 1914 (XVI-XVIII), May 21-26, 1914 (Ch. XIX-XXIII).

The Adventures of Prickly Porky: May 28-30, 1912 (Ch. I-III), Aug. 10-Sept. 1, 1914 (Ch. IV-XXIII).

The Adventures of Old Man Coyote: June 10-July 9, 1913.

The Adventures of Paddy the Beaver: Nov. 5-Dec. 1, 1913.

The Adventures of Poor Mrs. Quack: Mar. 20-Apr. 13., 1916 (Ch. I-XVIII), Apr. 22, 1916 (Ch. XIX), May 1, 1916 (Ch. XX).

The Adventures of Bobby Coon: Mar. 5-14, 1917 (Ch. I-IX), Mar. 21-23, 1917 (Ch. X-XII), Mar. 27-Apr. 10, 1917 (Ch. XIII-XXIII).

The Adventures of Jimmy Skunk: May 17-30, 1916 (Ch. I-XI), June 11-23, 1917 (Ch. XII-XXIII).

The Adventures of Bob White: Sept. 20-Oct. 23, 1915 (Ch. I-XXI), Oct. 30, 1915 (Ch. XXII).

The Adventures of Ol' Mistah Buzzard: July 11-13, 1912 (Ch. I-III), July 17, 1912 (Ch. IV), July 30-Aug. 18, 1917 (Ch. V-XXII), Mar. 18-19, 1914 (Ch. XXIV-XXV).

Green Meadow Series

Happy Jack: Nov. 21-Dec. 4, 1912 Ch. I-XII), Feb. 10-Mar. 5, 1915 (Ch. XIII-XXXIII).

Mrs. Peter Rabbit: July 10-Aug. 9, 1913 (Ch. I-XXVII), Aug. 25-29, 1913 (Ch. XXVIII-XXXII).

Bowser the Hound: Jan. 11-Mar. 1, 1919.

Old Granny Fox: Jan. 4-8, 1916 (Ch. I-V), Feb. 17-21, 1914 (Ch. VI-X), Jan. 9-Jan. 26, 1917 (Ch. XI-XXVI), Sept. 23, 1912 (Ch. XXVII), Sept. 26, 1912 (Ch. XXVIII), Oct. 10, 1912 (Ch. XXIX).

Green Forest Series

Lightfoot the Deer: Oct. 19, 1916 (Ch. IV), Oct. 29-Dec. 9, 1919 (Ch. V-XL).
Blacky the Crow: July 13-17, 1916 (Ch. XXIX-XXXII).
Whitefoot the Wood Mouse: Apr. 29-May 7, 1919 (Ch. I-VIII).
Buster Bear's Twins: Mar. 31-May 16, 1921.

Smiling Pool Series

Billy Mink: Dec. 10-22, 1919 (Ch. I-XI), Jan. 6-Feb. 7, 1920 (Ch. XII-XL).
Jerry Muskrat at Home: Sept. 18-Oct. 31, 1918 (Ch. I-XXXIII),Dec. 26-30, 1919 (Ch. XXXV-XXXVIII).
Longlegs the Heron: Aug. 21-23, 1916 (Ch. I-III), July 18-Aug. 13, 1921 (Ch. IV-XXVII).

The Burgess Bird Book for Children

The Burgess Bird Book for Children: May 12-Sept. 27, 1919.

Books Copyrighted in 1914 by J. N. Cole, Jr.

Buster Bear Invites Old Mr. Toad to Dine: May 20, 1914.
Busy Folks and Sleepy Folks: Nov. 25, 1914.
Danny Meadow Mouse Learns Something: Apr. 23, 1912.
The Digging Match: Mar. 19, 1912.
The Discontent of Peter Rabbit: May 13, 1913.
The Feast at the Big Rock: Mar. 6, 1912.
Four Little Mice at School and Play: July 6, 1914.
Fun With Farmer Brown's Boy: May 11, 1912.
A Glad Time Made a Sad Time: Nov. 27, 1914.
An Important Meeting at the Smiling Pool: Nov. 3, 1914.
Jack Frost Helps Paddy the Beaver: Dec. 8, 1913.
Jerry Muskrat Begins to Build: Aug. 10, 1912.
Jerry Muskrat is Laughed At: Aug. 8, 1912.
Jerry Muskrat Wins Respect: Aug. 9, 1912.
Johnny Chuck Loses His Temper: Apr. 19, 1912.
Jumper the Hare Cannot Sleep: Apr. 18, 1914.
Mr. Toad and Danny Meadow Mouse Take a Walk: Apr. 21, 1912.
Old Mr. Toad Gets His Stomach Full: May 21, 1914.
Paddy the Beaver Gives Warning: Nov. 1, 1913.
Peter Rabbit Has Hard Work to Believe His Eyes: Apr. 8, 1914.
Peter Rabbit Introduces His Big Cousin: Apr. 12, 1912.
Peter Rabbit is Lonesome: July 10, 1913.
Peter Rabbit Learns from Striped Chipmunk: Nov. 16, 1914.
Peter Rabbit Puts on Airs: May 16, 1913.
The Strange Tracks in the Green Forest: Mar. 7, 1914.

131

Striped Chipmunk Has a Secret: Nov. 14, 1914.
Striped Chipmunk's Secret Joke: Nov. 13, 1914.
Unc' Billy Possum Has a Fright: Nov. 28, 1914.

Books Published in 1924 by John H. Eggers

Baby Possum's Queer Voyage: Aug. 3, 1912.
Digger the Badger Decides to Stay: June 18, 1912.
Grandfather Frog Gets a Ride: May 13, 1912.
A Great Joke on Jimmy Skunk: Jan. 17, 1913.
Happy Jack Squirrel Helps Unc' Billy: Mar. 1, 1913.
The Neatness of Bobby Coon: May 29, 1912.

Books Published in 1928 by John H. Eggers

Baby Possum Has a Scare: Aug. 2, 1912.
Bowser the Hound Meets His Match: June 20, 1912.
Grandfather Frog Fools Farmer Brown's Boy: May 14, 1912.
Peter Rabbit Learns to Use His New Coat: Jan. 16, 1913.
Happy Jack Squirrel's Bright Idea: Mar. 3, 1913.
Bobby Coon Has A Good Time: May 30, 1912.

Cubby Bear Books

A Frightened Baby: Aug. 16-17, 1927.
Farmer Brown's Boy Becomes Curious: Aug. 18-19, 1927.
What Farmer Brown's Boy Did: Aug. 20, 22, 1927.
Cubby Bear Has a Mind of His Own: Aug. 23-24, 1927.
An Imp of Mischief: Aug. 26, 29, 1927.
Cubby in Mother Brown's Pantry: Aug. 30-31, 1927.
A Woe-Begone Little Bear: Sept. 1-2, 1927.
Cubby Gets a Bath: Sept. 3, 5, 1927.
Milk and Honey: Sept. 6-7, 1927.
Cubby Finds an Open Door: Sept. 8-9, 1927.

Books Published by Samuel Lowe Co.

What Mr. Toad Did With His Old Suit: Mar. 21, 1912.
Everybody Lends Jerry Muskrat a Hand: Aug. 12, 1912.

NOTES ON FOREIGN EDITIONS OF BOOKS
BY THORNTON W. BURGESS

Burgess stories have been translated into the languages of many countries around the world. The following list of Burgess books published in foreign countries, noted during the compilation of this bibliography, is not intended to be exhaustive.

CANADA

McClelland and Stewart Limited, Toronto, publishers
Books published simultaneously with the U.S. Little, Brown editions.

> The Burgess Seashore Book for Children - 1929
> The Wishing-Stone Stories - 1935
> Tales From the Storyteller's House - 1938
> While the Story-Log Burns - 1939
> Nature Story Books, all 6 vols. - 1944-1950

Bedtime Story-Books, French trans., illus. by Courtis Westland, 1948, paper covers, b&w illus., full-col. cover illus. (La Nature en Histoire).

> Les Aventures de Goupil le Renard (The Adventures of Reddy Fox)
> Les Aventures de Grand Moquer (The Adventures of Mr. Mocker)
> Les Aventures de Jeannot Lapin (The Adventures of Peter Cottontail)
> Les Aventures de L'Oncle Azor Opossum (The Adventures of Unc' Billy Possum)
> Les Aventures de Siffleux Marmotte (The Adventures of Johnny Chuck)

Oxford University Press, Toronto
Animal Stories, illus. by Harrison Cady, 1942. (pub. in U.S. by Platt & Munk).

Blue Ribbon Books, Toronto
Story Book, illus. by Nino Carbe, 1954 (pub. in U.S. by Garden City Books).

Little, Brown & Company, Toronto
Little, Brown of Toronto published several of the books simultaneously with the United States editions.

> Aunt Sally's Friends in Fur - 1955
> Now I Remember - 1960
> Bedtime Stories - 1960 (pub. in U.S. by Grosset & Dunlap)
> Old Mother West Wind, Golden Anniversary Ed. - 1960
> Mother West Wind's Children, New Illustrated Ed. - 1962
> Mother West Wind's Neighbors, New Illustated Ed. - 1968

> The Adventures of Peter Cottontail, the one member of the Bedtime Story-Books noted, has a cover illus. and end papers (blue)by Harrison Cady, one b&w plate and several b&w illus. that are imitations of Cady, 1964.

Grosset & Dunlap
Books published simultaneously with the U.S Grosset & Dunlap editions.

> The Burgess Bird Book for Children - 1965
> The Burgess Animal Book for Children - 1965

GREAT BRITAIN

John Lane, The Bodley Head, London, publisher
Bedtime Story-Books, illus. by Harrison Cady. Same format as Little, Brown editions, with covers of different colors. The members of the series that came out in 1938, 1939, and 1940 have "The Adventures of" deleted from the titles.

> The Adventures of Buster Bear - 1931
> The Adventures of Chatterer the Red Squirrel - 1931
> The Adventures of Grandfather Frog - 1931
> The Adventures of Paddy the Beaver - 1931
> The Adventures of Peter Cottontail - 1931
> The Adventures of Reddy Fox - 1931
> The Adventures of Old Mr. Toad - 1932
> The Adventures of Poor Mrs. Quack - 1932
> The Adventures of Prickly Porky - 1932
> The Adventures of Sammy Jay - 1932
> Jimmy Skunk - 1938
> Johnny Chuck - 1938
> Mr. Mocker - 1938
> Old Man Coyote - 1938
> Bobby Coon - 1939
> Danny Meadow Mouse - 1939
> Bob White - 1940
> Unc' Billy Possum - 1940

Green Forest Series, all four volumes - 1933

Green Meadow Series, all four volumes - 1934

Smiling Pool Series, all four volumes - 1935

Mother West Wind Series

> Old Mother West Wind - 1937
> Mother West Wind's Children - 1937
> Mother West Wind's Animal Friends - 1937
> Mother West Wind's Neighbours - 1937
> Mother West Wind "Why" Stories - 1950
> Mother West Wind "How" Stories - 1950
> Mother West Wind "When" Stories - 1950
> Mother West Wind "Where" Stories - 1950

Tales from the Storyteller's House, illus. by L. Palmer, 1938

While the Story-Log Burns, illus. by L. Palmer, 1939

Paddy the Beaver Builds a Dam (Chapters I-III, & V of *The Adventures of Paddy the Beaver*, Boston, Little, Brown, 1917), 20p., 14cm., paper covers.

MacDonald & Company, London, publisher

The Adventures of Peter Cottontail, illus. by Phoebe Erickson (pub. in U.S. by Grosset & Dunlap in 1958).

Bedtime Stories, illus. by Carl and Mary Hauge - 1960 (pub. in U.S. by Grosset & Dunlap in 1959).

FRANCE

Éditions de la Paix, Paris & Brussels

Bedtime Story-Books. French versions of the New Illustrated Editions of 1941 & 1944. Illustrated by Harrison Cady. Translated by H. de Beaune, paper covers. (Les Veillées Enfantines)

> Les Aventures de Courte-Queue le Champagnol (The Adventures of Danny Meadow Mouse), c.1947.
> Les Aventures de Grand-Père Grenouille (The Adventures of Grandfather Frog), c.1947.
> Les Aventures de Guillaume la Skonks (The Adventures of Jimmy Skunk), c.1947.
> Les Aventures de Bruin L'Ours (The Adventures of Buster Bear), c.1948.
> Les Aventures de Dodo la Marmotte (The Adventures of Johnny Chuck), c.1948.
> Les Aventures de Roux le Renard (The Adventures of Reddy Fox), c.1948.

Les Éditions denoël et Steele, Paris

Bedtime Story-Books (La Clef de Champs)

> Les Aventures de Patternouse le Renard (The Adventures of Reddy Fox). Trans. by Marie-Louise Bataille. Illus. by Prybil.
> Les Aventures de Jeannot Lapin (The Adventures of Peter Cottontail). Trans. by Marie-Louise Bataille. Illus. by Prybil.
> Les Aventures de Rainette la Grenouille (The Adventures of Grandfather Frog). Trans. by Jan Pan. Illus. by Prybil.
> Les Aventures de Martin le Gros Ours (The Adventures of Buster Bear). Trans. by Jan Pan. Illus. by Prybil.

Éditions RST, Mulhouse, France

Tous les Amis de Jeannot Lapin. Illus. by C. & M. Hauge and P. Erickson. [Mulhouse], Éditions RST, 1960. 68p., col. illus. A translation of *The Adventures of Peter Cottontail.*

SWEDEN

Albert Bonniers Förlag, Stockholm, publishers

Mor Vastanvind (Old Mother West Wind). Translated by Marianne Larsson. Stockholm, Albert Bonniers Förlag, 1939.

CHINA

Kuang Hsuch Pub. House, Shanghai

Mother West Wind's Animal Friends. Illus. by George Kerr. Trans. into Chinese by K. E. Wood. Shanghai, Kuang Hsuch Pub. House, 1921. (Title page in English, text in Chinese.)

NOTES ON CHILDREN'S LITERATURE
ANTHOLOGIES CONTAINING BURGESS STORIES

Stories by Thornton W. Burgess have been included in several anthologies of children's literature. During the compilation of this bibliography, note was made of any discovered and are listed here, including, in most cases, the name of the story and the source if it came from a Burgess book. The anthologies are listed in order of publication.

The Wide Awake Fourth Reader. By Clara Murray. Boston, Little, Brown, 1914. (Clara Murray is the pseudonym of Etta Austin Blaisdell McDonald.)
"Little Joe Otter's Slippery Slide" [from *Old Mother West Wind*]
"Peter Rabbit Plays a Joke" [from *Old Mother West Wind*]

Bedtime Stories Club. Souvenir Magazine of Our First Club Meeting. Sept. 30, 1915. Edited by Horace Tibbs. n.p., *The Globe and Advertizer,* 1915.
"Peter Rabbit's Get Acquainted Party," pp. 3-5.

John Martin's Big Book, 1919 [cited in Dowhan magazine bibliography].
"Little Camp Sharp Eyes"

John Martin's Big Book, 1920 [cited in Dowhan magazine bibliography].
"A Million Little Sunbeams"

Anthology of Children's Literature. Comp. by Edna Johnson and Carrie Scott. [1st ed.] New York, Houghton-Mifflin, 1935.
In the section entitled "Nature Stories" are selections from *The Adventures of Old Mr. Toad.*
"Peter Rabbit Finds Old Mr. Toad," p. 460. (Chapter IV)
"Old Mr. Toad's Music Bag," p. 461. (Chapter V)
"Old Mr. Toad's Babies," p. 462. (Chapter VIII)
"The Smiling Pool Kindergarten," p. 463. (Chapter IX)
"Old Mr. Toad Shows His Tongue," p. 464. (Chapter XII)

——Comp. by Edna Johnson, Carrie E. Scott, and Evelyn Sickels. Illus. by N. C. Wyeth. [2nd ed.] New York, Houghton-Mifflin, 1948.
In the section entitled "Non-Fiction, Nature" are:
"Old Mr. Toad's Music Bag," p. 576.
"Old Mr. Toad Shows His Tongue," p. 577.

A Child's Treasury of Stories. New York and Sandusky, Ohio, The American
Crayon Company, c.1942, 1943, 1946. (An Old Faithful Book)
> In the section entitled "Burgess Famous Bed Time Stories" are:
> "How Reddy Fox Was Surprised" [from *Old Mother West Wind*]
> "Reddy Fox, The Boaster" [from *Mother West Wind's Children*]
> "Reddy Fox Barks at the Moon" [from *Mother West Wind's Children*]
> (There may be others. Copy examined is incomplete.)

The Golden Almanac.   By Dorothy Bennett. Pictures by Masha. New York,
Simon & Schuster, 1944.
> "Danny Meadow Mouse Plays Hide and Seek" [Chapter III of *The Adventures of Danny
> Meadow Mouse*]

The Child's World. Vol. I *Stories of Childhood.* Edited by Esther M. Bjoland.
Chicago, The Child's World, Inc., 1947.
> In the section entitled "Nature Stories" are two stories from *The Adventures of Old Mr.
> Toad:*
> "Peter Rabbit Finds Old Mr. Toad," p. 186 (Chapter IV)
> "Old Mr. Toad's Music Bag," p. 189 (Chapter V)

Bedtime Tales. Edited by Hazel Packard. New York, Simon and Schuster,
1948. [cited in Neu bibliography].

Golden Book of Nursery Tales. Edited by Elsa Jane Werner. New York, Simon
and Schuster, 1950. (A Big Golden Book) [cited in Neu bibliography].

*Storytime Tales; A Treasury of 42 Favorite Stories, Poems, and Songs, Old and
New.* Pictures by Corinne Malvern. New York, Simon and Schuster, 1950.
(A Big Golden Book.)
> In the section entitled "Favorite Animal Stories" is:
> "The Most Beautiful Thing in the World," pp. 124-128 [from *Old Mother West
> Wind*]

*The Second Child Life Story Book: New Read Aloud Stories from Child Life
Magazine.* Adelaide Field, ed. Philadelphia, John C. Winston Co., 1953.
> "The Wonderful Good Feeling Day," pp. 64-68.

The Illustrated Treasury of Children's Literature. Edited and with an introduction by Margaret E. Martignoni. New York, Grosset & Dunlap, 1955.
> "Two Happy Little Bears," pp. 43-45. Illus. by Phoebe Erickson.
> "Peter Finds a Name," pp. 307-308. Illus. by Harrison Cady. [from Chap. II of *The
> Adventures of Peter Cottontail*]

My Book House, Vol. 3 *Up One Pair of Stairs.* Ed. by Olive Beaupré Miller.
Lake Bluff, Ill., The Book House for Children, 1956.
> "Peter Rabbit Decides to Change His Name," pp. 49-58. [Chap. I-III of *The Adventures
> of Peter Cottontail*] 9 illus. by M. D.

Best in Children's Books. Garden City, N.Y., Nelson Doubleday, Inc., 1959.
> "Unc Billy Possum," pp. 117-123.

CHRONOLOGY OF BOOKS BY
THORNTON W. BURGESS

Series abbreviations:

Mother West Wind Series (MWW)
Boy Scout Series (BS)
The Bedtime Story-Books (BSB)
Green Meadow Series (GM)
Burgess Natural History Books
   for Children (NH)

Green Forest Series (GF)
Smiling Pool Series (SP)
Little Color Classics (LCC)
Books of Nature Stories (NS)
Wonder Books (WB)
Wonder Read Aloud Books (WRA)

1905 The Bride's Primer

1910 Old Mother West Wind
     (MWW)

1911 Mother West Wind's Children
     (MWW)

1912 The Boy Scouts of Woodcraft
     Camp (BS)

     Mother West Wind's Animal
     Friends (MWW)

1913 The Boy Scouts on Swift River
     (BS)

     The Adventures of Reddy Fox
     (BSB)

     The Adventures of Johnny Chuck
     (BSB)

     Mother West Wind's Neighbors
     (MWW)

     Little Animal Stories for Little
     Children

     The Joy of the Beautiful Pine

1914 The Adventures of Peter
     Cottontail (BSB)

     The Adventures of Unc' Billy
     Possum (BSB)

     The Boy Scouts on Lost Trail (BS)

     The Bedtime Story Calendar
     (for 1915)

     The Adventures of Jerry Muskrat
     (BSB)

     The Adventures of Mr. Mocker
     (BSB)

     32 miniature books, c.J.N.Cole

1915 The Adventures of Danny Meadow
     Mouse (BSB)

     The Adventures of Grandfather
     Frog (BSB)

     The Adventures of Chatterer
     the Red Squirrel (BSB)

     The Adventures of Sammy Jay
     (BSB)

     Mother West Wind 'Why' Stories
     (MWW)

Little Stories for Bedtime

My Own Bedtime Story

Tommy and the Wishing-Stone

The Boy Scouts in a Trapper's
Camp (BS)

1916 The Adventures of Buster Bear
(BSB)

The Adventures of Old Mr. Toad
(BSB)

Mother West Wind 'How' Stories
(MWW)

The Adventures of Old Man Coyote
(BSB)

The Adventures of Prickly Porky
(BSB)

1917 The Adventures of Paddy the
Beaver (BSB)

The Adventures of Poor Mrs. Quack
(BSB)

Mother West Wind 'When' Stories
(MWW)

1918 Happy Jack Squirrel's Thrift Club

The Adventures of Bobby Coon
(BSB)

The Adventures of Jimmy Skunk
(BSB)

Mother West Wind 'Where' Stories
(MWW)

Happy Jack (GM)

1919 The Adventures of Bob White
(BSB)

The Adventures of Ol' Mistah
Buzzard (BSB)

Mrs. Peter Rabbit (GM)

The Burgess Bird Book for
Children (NH)

1920 Bowser the Hound (GM)

Old Granny Fox (GM)

The Burgess Animal Book for
Children (NH)

Peter Rabbit Book

1921 Lightfoot the Deer (GF)

1922 Blacky the Crow (GF)

Whitefoot the Wood Mouse (GF)

1923 The Burgess Flower Book for
Children (NH)

Buster Bear's Twins (GF)

1924 Billy Mink (SP)

Set of 6 books pub. by Eggers

1925 4 books pub. by Saalfield Pub.

Little Joe Otter (SP)

1926 Jerry Muskrat at Home (SP)

The Christmas Reindeer

1927 Longlegs the Heron (SP)

Set of 6 books pub. by Eggers

1929 Cubby Bear Books

The Burgess Seashore Book for
Children (NH)

Wild Flowers We Know

Wild Flowers We Should Know

1933 Birds You Should Know

6 miniature books pub. by
Whitman

1935 Wah Wah Taysee

1937 The Book of Animal Life

Tales from the Storyteller's
House

1938 Mother Nature's Song and Story
Book

While the Story-Log Burns

1940 Thornton Burgess Animal Library

1941 Little Pete's Adventure (LCC)

Little Burgess Bird Book for
Children

Little Burgess Animal Book for
Children

1942 Little Red's Adventure (LCC)

Little Chuck's Adventure (LCC)

1944 Why Peter Rabbit's Ears Are Long

On the Green Meadows (NS)

1945 At the Smiling Pool (NS)

1946 The Crooked Little Path (NS)

1947 The Dear Old Briar Patch (NS)

1949 Baby Animal Stories
Nature Almanac
Along Laughing Brook (NS)

1950 At Paddy the Beaver's Pond (NS)
A Thornton Burgess Picture
Story-Book

1954 Peter Rabbit and Reddy Fox (WB)
The Thornton W. Burgess Story
Coloring Book
The Littlest Christmas Tree (WB)

1955 Aunt Sally's Friends in Fur

1956 Little Peter Cottontail (WB)

1957 How Peter Cottontail Got His
Name (WB)

1958 Read Aloud Peter Rabbit Stories
(WRA)

1959 Nature Stories to Read Aloud
(WRA)

1960 Now I Remember

1963 The Million Little Sunbeams

1965 The Burgess Book of Nature Lore
Mother West Wind Stories to
Read Aloud (WRA)

A CHECKLIST OF SOURCES ON
THORNTON W. BURGESS AND HIS WORKS

This list, while not intended to be exhaustive, contains books and articles on the life of Burgess, his writings, and genealogies of his family. It does not contain brief articles from encyclopedias and other reference books or local newpaper articles.

Beckley, Zoe. "Why [sic] Is Thornton W. Burgess?" *Peoples Home Journal* (July 1929), pp. 14-15 + .

"Bedtime Man." *New Yorker*, 16 (Oct. 26, 1940), 16.

Blake, Fran. "Meet Thornton W. Burgess' Lovable Aunt Sally. In Real Life Famous Bedtime Story Character is 90-Year-Old Cape Codder," *Boston Sunday Globe* (Mar. 16, 1952). (Cited by Russel A. Lovell in *The Cape Cod Story of Thornton W. Burgess*, 1974, p. 93.)

Brown, Meribah K. "Springfield Children Know Their Authors," *Wilson Library Bulletin*, 17 (May 1943), 710-711. (Brief mention of Burgess and a photo.)

Bryan, J., III. "Mother Nature's Apostle," *Saturday Review of Literature*, 23 (Dec. 14, 1940), 11-13.

    Reprinted under title "Mother Nature's Brother," *Reader's Digest*, 38 (Jan.1941), 114-116.

    Reprinted under title "Mother Nature's Brother," *Saturday Review Gallery*, selected by Jerome Beatty, Jr. New York, Simon & Schuster, 1959, pp. 338-344.

Burgess, Ebenezer. *Burgess Genealogy: Memorial of the Family of Thomas and Dorothy Burgess, Who were Settled at Sandwich in the Plymouth Colony in 1637*. Boston, T. R. Marvin & Son, 1865. (Includes Charles Burgess and his six children, the third being Thornton W., the author's father.)

"Burgess Publishes 10,000 Nature Stories." *Publisher's Weekly*, 145 (Feb. 5, 1944), 689.

"The Burgess Radio Nature League." *Literary Digest*, 85 (June 6, 1925), 30.

Burgess, Thornton W. Article in *Cape Cod Compass* (Aug. 1956). (Cited by Lovell.)

——*Aunt Sally's Friends in Fur; or the Woodhouse Night Club.* Boston, Little, Brown, 1955.

——"The Gold Mine I Discovered When I Was 35," *American Magazine,* 87 (May 1919), 36 + .

——"Making Men of Them," *Good Housekeeping,* 59 (July 1914), 2-8.

——"Nature as the Universal Teacher," *Natural History,* 22 (Mar. - Apr. 1922), 137.

——*Now I Remember; Autobiography of an Amateur Naturalist.* Boston, Little, Brown, 1960.

——"One Day in a Fisherman's Life," *Outdoor America,* 3 (Apr. 1925), 20.

——"Writing Stories for a Million Children," *The Rotarian* (Mar. 1923), pp. 135-137 + .

Carlson, Patricia. "Thornton Burgess; An Author with a Naturalistic Point of View," Unpublished term paper, Keene State College, Keene, N.H., Mar. 31, 1969. (Cited by Lovell.)

Devlin, John C. and Grace Naismith. *The World of Roger Tory Peterson; An Authorized Biography.* Foreword by Elliot Richardson. New York, Times Books, 1977. (Burgess mentioned on pp. 66-67. Little, Brown turned down Peterson's *A Field Guide to the Birds* since they were planning to publish Burgess's *Birds You Should Know.*)

Dowhan, Michael, Jr. *Thornton W. Burgess: A Magazine Bibliography.* Williamstown, Mass., printed by Chapel Hill Press, 1977.

Fox, Dorothea Magdalene. "Thornton Burgess Recalls a 90-Year Romance with Nature," *Audubon Magazine,* 66 (Sept. - Oct. 1964), 312-313.

Froman, Robert. "Thornton Burgess: Peter Rabbit's Godfather," *Coronet* (Nov. 1947), 146-150.

Furman, Lucy. "The Woodhouse Night Club," *Nature Magazine,* 41 (Oct. 1948), 409-411.

Harris, Arthur S., Jr. "Bedtime Story Man," *Nature Magazine,* 49 (Jan. 1956), 17-19 + .

——"He Gave Us Peter Rabbit," *Hometown; the Rexall Magazine* (July 1958), pp. 6-7.

Hubbard, C. T. "The Mice That Sing," *Yankee,* 33 (Oct. 1969), 98-99 + . (Burgess discussed on p. 132.)

"Is This a Fair Deal?" *Reader's Digest,* 38 (Feb. 1941), 127.

Kenney, Harry C. "Neighbor Burgess," *Christian Science Monitor* (Jan. 10, 1948), pp. 8-9.

Kunitz, Stanley Jasspon, and Howard Haycraft. "Thornton W. Burgess" in *The Junior Book of Authors.* New York, H. W. Wilson, 1934, pp. 70-71.

Krutch, Joseph Wood. "A Natural World of Make-Believe," *Saturday Review*, 43 (Sept. 24, 1960), 18.

"Life Visits the Bedtime-Story Man at Laughing Brook." *Life*, 17 (Aug. 28, 1944), 99-102. (Cited by Lovell as "The Triumph of the Puritan Spirit.")

Levine, Louis. "Unforgettable Thornton W. Burgess," *Reader's Digest*, 91 (Oct. 1967), 100-105.

Lovell, Russell A., Jr. *The Cape Cod Story of Thornton W. Burgess*. With an extensive bibliography of Burgess's books prepared by Ralph M. Titcomb. Sandwich, Mass., Thornton W. Burgess Centennial Committee, 1974.

"The Man Who Made Children Love Bedtime." *Saturday Review of Literature*, 15, Section 2 (Mar. 27, 1937), 16A.

Meigs, Cornelia, Anne Thaxter Eaton, Elizabeth Nesbitt, and Ruth Hill Viquers. *A Critical History of Children's Literature*. New York, The MacMillan Co., 1953. (Burgess discussed on p.368.)

Nash, Ogden. "Mr. Burgess, Meet Mr. Barmecide," *New Yorker*, 30 (Jan. 1 1955), 26. poem.

Neu, John, comp. "A Bibliography of Thornton Burgess," Compiled privately for the University of Wisconsin Memorial Library, Madison, Wisconsin, about 1959.

Nordell, Rod. "The Burgess World of Animals and Children; A Golden Anniversary by the Laughing Brook," *Christian Science Monitor*, Eastern ed., 52 (Sept. 15, 1960), 11.

Nye, George Hyatt, and Frank E. Best. *A Genealogy of the Nye Family*. Edited by David Fisher Nye. Chicago, The Nye Family of America Association, 1907. (Burgess's great-grandfather, Daniel Butler Nye, and his grandparents, Charles and Anne Swift (Nye) Burgess, are listed on p. 272.)

Nye, L. Bert, Jr., comp. *A Genealogy of American Nyes of English Origin*. Vol. I. Generations 1 through 8. East Sandwich, Mass., The Nye Family of America Association, 1977. (Thornton W. Burgess is listed on p. 467 under his grandmother Anne Swift (Nye) Burgess as the only child of her son Thornton Waldo.)

Obituary. *Library Journal*, 90 (Sept. 15, 1965), 3715.
——*New York Times* (June 6, 1965), 84.
——*Newsweek*, 65 (June 21, 1965), 90.
——*Publisher's Weekly*, 187 (June 14, 1965), 80.
——*Time*, 85 (June 18, 1965), 20.

O'Donnell, Richard W. "The Home of Peter Rabbit." Illustrations by Martin R. Ahearn. *Ford Times*, 71 (Apr. 1978), 61-64.

One Hundred and Twenty-Five Years of Publishing, 1837-1962. Boston, Little, Brown, 1962. (Burgess is mentioned on pp. 65-66.)

"One Man's Kingdom." *Newsweek,* 56 (Sept. 26, 1960), 122.

O'Neill, Paul. "Fifty Years on the Green Meadows," *Life,* 49 (Nov. 14, 1960), 112-114.

Rood, Ronald. *The Loon in My Bathtub.* Brattleboro, Vermont, Stephen Greene Press, 1964. (Burgess's influence on Rood is discussed in Chapter 1, "Blame Mr. Burgess.")

Roth, Charles E. "Foreword" to *Mother West Wind's Neighbors* by Thornton W. Burgess. New Illustrated Edition. Boston, Little, Brown, 1968.

Saltford, Herb. "A Man, His Dream and a Happy Ending," *Yankee,* 37 (June, 1973), 94-97 + .

Shepherd, William G. "The Bedtime Story Man," *Red Cross Magazine,* 15 (May 1920), 14-17.

Spies, Joseph R. *The Compleat Cat.* New York, Bonanza Books, 1966. A discussion of Burgess is included, p.17.

Tante, Dilly (pseud.). *Living Authors.* New York, H. W. Wilson Co., 1931. ("Thornton Waldo Burgess" on pp. 58-59.)

"Thornton W. Burgess and His Nature Stories for Children." *Publisher's Weekly,* 168 (July 23, 1955), 316-317.

"Thornton W. Burgess Centennial Celebration Souvenir Program, 1874-1974." Held Sandwich, Mass. Aug. 8, 9, 10, 1974.

Thornton W. Burgess, The Bedtime Story Man. Compliments of Little, Brown, & Company, about 1925, 24 p. incl. cover. ("The Story of Thornton W. Burgess," pp. 3-8, "An Appreciation of Thornton W. Burgess," pp. 9-20, "The Books of Thornton W. Burgess," pp. 21-24.

Walsh, Lavinia. "Million Children Would 'Choose' Him for President — at Bedtime, *Cape Cod Magazine and Cape Cod Life* (Aug. 15, 1927), pp. 7-8 + . ("Boys from the Cape Who Have Made Good," #IV, Thornton W. Burgess.)

Waterman, Donald Lines. *The Waterman Family.* 3 vols. New Haven, Conn., Tuttle, Morehouse & Taylor, 1939. (Charles Cotesworth Pinckney Waterman, Burgess's mother's uncle, with whom the author lived as a child, is mentioned in Vol. 2, p. 235. Burgess's mother and grandmother are not mentioned.)

"When Do We Eat?" *The Outlook,* 130 (Mar. 1, 1922), 330-331. (Cited by Burgess in *Now I Remember* (1960), p. 223 as "When Does Old Man Coyote Eat." Burgess said his reply was printed in the next issue.)

Worcester Telegram (Jan. 15, 1961), (Cited by Lovell as the article Burgess felt was the best on himself.)

Wright, Wayne W. "The World of Thornton W. Burgess; An Introduction and Descriptive Bibliography," Unpublished graduate seminar paper in the History of Children's Literature in America, School of Library and Information Science, State University of New York at Albany, Dec. 16, 1974.

"Writes Stories for the Kiddies." *Cape Cod and All the Pilgrim Land,* 4 (June 1920), 13-14.

ARTISTS' CONCEPTIONS OF PETER RABBIT

Thornton W. Burgess's most beloved character, Peter Rabbit, has been depicted by many artists through the years. Shown here are various Peters — both fanciful and life-like — as they appeared in Burgess books.

GEORGE KERR drew Peter in 1910 for Burgess's first animal book *Old Mother West Wind* (Boston, Little, Brown, c.1910, 1914, renewed 1938, c.1960). Kerr started the tradition of the Burgess characters wearing clothes.

(Left) HARRISON CADY, the most famous of all the Burgess book illustrators, drew Peter Rabbit for the books for over 50 years. This 1914 Peter is from *The Adventures of Peter Cottontail* (Boston, Little, Brown, c.1914, renewed 1942 by Thornton W. Burgess). (Right) In the same picture redrawn by Cady for the 1950 Grosset & Dunlap edition of *The Adventures of Peter Cottontail*, Peter has a slimmer look.

Sometimes Peter dressed more casually, as in this Cady illustration from *On the Green Meadows* (Boston, Little, Brown, 1944).

The nature artist LOUIS AGASSIZ FUERTES painted Peter as a life-like rabbit in *The Burgess Animal Book for Children* (Boston, Little, Brown, c.1920, renewed 1948 by Thornton W. Burgess).

Peter by NINA R. JORDAN in *What Farmer Brown's Boy Did*, a Cubby Bear Book (Racine, Wis., Whitman Pub. Co., c.1927, illustrations c. 1929).

An unnamed illustrator copied Harrison Cady's Peter for the cover illustration of *Peter Rabbit's Carrots* (Racine, Wis., Whitman Pub. Co., c.1933).

(Above) PHOEBE ERICKSON gave Peter a natural, young look in *Baby Animal Stories* (New York, Grosset & Dunlap, 1949). (Right) NINO CARBE drew this Peter used in *What Mr. Toad Did With His Old Suit* (New York, Samuel Lowe Co., c.1953 James and Jonathan).

Peter Rabbit by CARL and MARY HAUG from inside front cover of *Peter Rabbit an Reddy Fox* (New York, Wonder Book c.1957).

PAULINE JACKSON'S distinguished looking Peter Rabbit from
How Peter Cottontail Got His Name (New York, Wonder Books,
c.1957).

ELIZABETH MONATH drew this Peter for the title page of *Read
Aloud Peter Rabbit Stories* (New York, Wonder Books, c.1958).

TITLE INDEX

This index lists titles of books and series by Thornton W. Burgess. Principal descriptions and citations are noted in boldface print. Secondary references are in regular print. References to illustrations appear at the end of each listing.